365
Days *of* Biblical Insight

365
Days *of* Biblical Insight

J.D. Glass

TATE PUBLISHING & *Enterprises*

365 Days of Biblical Insight
Copyright © 2010 by Jonathan Glass. All rights reserved.

No part of this publication may be reproduced, stored in a retrieval system or transmitted in any way by any means, electronic, mechanical, photocopy, recording or otherwise without the prior permission of the author except as provided by USA copyright law.

Scripture quotations marked (AMP) are taken from the Amplified Bible, Copyright © 1954, 1958, 1962, 1964, 1965, 1987 by The Lockman Foundation. Used by permission.

Scripture quotations marked (GNT) are from the Good News Translation in Today's English Version- Second Edition Copyright © 1992 by American Bible Society. Used by Permission.

Scripture quotations marked (NIV) are takenfrom the Holy Bible, New International Version®. niv®. Copyright© 1973, 1978, 1984 by International Bible Society. Used by permission of Zondervan. All rights reserved.

Scripture quotations marked (NLT) are taken from the Holy Bible, New Living Translation, copyright © 1996. Used by permission of Tyndale House Publishers, Inc., Wheaton, Illinois 60189. All rights reserved.

The opinions expressed by the author are not necessarily those of Tate Publishing, LLC.

Published by Tate Publishing & Enterprises, LLC
127 E. Trade Center Terrace | Mustang, Oklahoma 73064 USA
1.888.361.9233 | www.tatepublishing.com

Tate Publishing is committed to excellence in the publishing industry. The company reflects the philosophy established by the founders, based on Psalm 68:11,
"The Lord gave the word and great was the company of those who published it."

Book design copyright © 2010 by Tate Publishing, LLC. All rights reserved.
Cover design by Brandon Wood
Interior design by Joey Garrett

Published in the United States of America

ISBN: 978-1-61663-432-2
Religion / Christian Life / Devotional
10.05.28

Dedication

This book is dedicated to everyone I love. My beloved God sent children. May you always be safe and have hearts brimming over with joy. To my wife, Michelle, may we always be. To my parents, without you both I never would have gotten so far. Thank you to everyone who played key roles in my spiritual development. I'll never forget a single one of you.

Introduction

If you have ever turned to the Bible for comfort in trying times, consider *365 Days of Biblical Insight* a highlight reel of the most comforting, challenging, and empowering verses in the Bible. However, there is a great deal more in this book than 365 selected verses. The Bible itself was written by divine inspiration, which inspired me to use my years of theological research to make the Bible easier to understand through original proverbs and beliefs that are tied closely to Scripture.

Undoubtedly, the Bible is a vast and mysterious book of laws, social obligations, and divine intervention. We are called to live our lives as Christ lived his. This means that we are to put a relationship with the Almighty above all else. However, telling a person to put God first without an explanation is like telling a person to be good, minus the how to. That is why this book was written, so that from the theological scholar to a person with a minimal knowledge of Scripture can come to a better understanding of God's will for their life.

I wrote *365 Days of Biblical Insight* because I wanted a closer, deeper understanding of the ways of the Lord. I am a student of life and believe that the bible is God's own word to humanity. Spending years of studying and applying God's Word to my experiences developed a desire to create literature that helps people draw from my experience strength and hope.

If religion is for those who are afraid of descending into the flames of perdition, then spirituality is for those who have already been. And for a long time, I've considered myself spiritual. Pain and suffering came to me at an early age, and after years of vexation, I began to make poor decisions for myself. Those poor decisions are what began my truest descent from God's protective hand. The years 1995–2003 were truly nightmarish.

Without going into detail, suffice it to say, I walked outside the lines of grace. I sinned intentionally until it no longer seemed wrong. In 1999 the darkness of this world had permeated my existence so deeply that I went to bed with horror on my mind and woke up to terror. I began to lose my will to fight and was indeed affected. Although I maintained my college classes, a job, and a relationship, people surely noticed that I was not who I once was. I needed deliverance.

In the spring of that year, deliverance appeared, and I was granted the energy to climb from perditions depths. By the time 2003 came, I had made significant progress, but still the Enemy had a grip on certain areas of my life. It was then that I had a near death experience in the middle of night. I woke up the next day feeling like I had been given a second chance and grabbed the opportunity to receive help.

Ever since, I have been receiving God's grace to be the man I have always wanted to be. In 2007 I got married to an amazing woman, and the next year we had a beautiful daughter named Arabella. The Glass family is currently expecting a son to be named Zachary; the name Zachary means spiritual, and Arabella means answer to a prayer. My life today is full of brightness and hope. I am living an existence in which my dreams are coming true, an existence which surpasses my wildest dreams. Thank you for being a part of it!

The most wonderful aspect to having seen the bottom is a true appreciation for growth and achievement. Just because I stopped making mistakes on purpose does not mean that I've gotten rid of all error. Life is about making progress every day, not perfection. And no matter how good I get at living life, there is no place on earth where anyone's exempt from trials and tribulation. Just when I thought that my teaching career and marriage were perfect, I found out that I was going to lose my job.

That was a huge hit to my security, but my wife and I persevered and found ways to adapt to life's curve balls. It turned out that the time I was off from work granted me great perspective into life and gave me an edge into writing the end to this book. Walt Disney once said, "Sometimes the best thing a man can get is a solid kick to the teeth." True, it hurts when it happens, but it tends to shake loose the preconceived notions as to how life should be lived and frees a soul to fly.

When tragedy strikes, in the darkness, is when a person discovers the substance of which he is truly made. Now I see it was no small favour the Lord granted me when he permitted calamity to come into my life, because all those trials and tribulations produced character in me, a personality that has made me able to withstand most anything. It is my prayer that this close-to-my-heart book blesses you as much as writing it has blessed me.

Enjoy and God bless.

January

January 1—Childlikeness

Most children are happy. Children don't try to figure life out; they simply observe and accept the truth as it presents itself. Adults who are childlike in nature and possess genuine curiosity will discover that the kingdom of heaven belongs to people just like them.

> At that time Jesus said, "I praise you, Father, Lord of heaven and earth, because you have hidden these things from the wise and learned, and revealed them to little children."
>
> Matthew 11:25 (NIV)

January 2—*Freedom*

In order to be free, you must be obedient. In order to be obedient, you must ask Christ to free you from selfishness. In order to be free from selfishness, you must suffer. Only through suffering can a person acquire true freedom. It's not an easy battle, but it is a fight worth the end result. There is nothing better than freedom.

> To the Jews who had believed him, Jesus said, "If you hold to my teaching, you are really my disciples. So if the Son sets you free, you will be free indeed."
>
> John 8:31, 36 (NIV)

January 3—Lambs among Wolves

Imagine swimming with sharks. Believers all over the world live this dangerous scenario every day as they interact with hateful people. And yet it is our privilege to keep hoping for a brighter day in which we will no longer be forced to combat the people who dwell in shadows. We are in the light no matter how dark things seem because the light of God dwells inside of our hearts.

> Go! I am sending you out like lambs among wolves.
>
> Luke 10:3 (NIV)

January 4—True Life

Surrendering your own wants and desires is a difficult thing. But when you put God first, you'll end up with everything you ever wanted.

> For whoever wants to save his life will lose it, but whoever loses his life for me will find it.
>
> Matthew 16:25 (NIV)

January 5—The Peace That Surpasses Understanding

Jesus gave us a gift before he went back to heaven. He gave us the peace that surpasses human understanding. For as long as we live, there will be times of trouble, but those trials and tribulations won't cause lasting harm. We can receive comfort from the Lord in times of trouble.

> Peace I leave with you; my peace I give you. I do not give to you as the world gives. Do not let your hearts be troubled and do not be afraid.
>
> John 14:27 (NIV)

January 6—True Freedom

The Lord gives freedom to his followers so that they can do what they should. Jesus said in his Sermon on the Mount, "Happy are those whose desire is to do what the Lord commands, for they will be fully satisfied." When you are living by faith and by spirit, you will undoubtedly feel a great sense of liberation.

> Now the Lord is the Spirit, and where the Spirit of the Lord is, there is freedom.
>
> 2 Corinthians 3:17 (NIV)

January 7—Citizenship

Being an American citizen is a great privilege. Many people sneak into America just to get a slave-wage job in order for their children to have hope and a future by being born here as citizens.

> The commander went to Paul and asked, "Tell me, are you a Roman citizen?" "Yes, I am," he answered. Then the commander said, "I had to pay a big price for my citizenship." "But I was born a citizen," Paul replied.
>
> Acts 22:27 (NIV)

January 8—A Matter of Life and Death

The Bible says, "fortunate are the children whose parents do what is good and right." The very idea of choosing death over life seems crazy. Who would choose to die? That's where temptation becomes a factor. The devil is man's opponent. He offers pleasure in return for our lives. Proverbs tells us, "knowledge and wisdom will give you pleasure and add years to your life." The only problem is that people want instant pleasure, and will inadvertently choose death to get it.

> This day I call heaven and earth as witnesses against you that I have set before you life and death, blessings and curses. Now choose life, so that you and your children may live and that you may love the LORD your God, listen to his voice, and hold fast to him. For the LORD is your life, and he will give you many years in the land he

swore to give to your fathers, Abraham, Isaac and Jacob.

> Deuteronomy 30:19–20 (NIV)

January 9—Testing

Why did God allow Satan to torment Job? It seems cruel, but somehow God saw fit to put his servant to the test. The Bible tells us that the Lord breaks us so that he can heal us, his way. Life is hard, but if you stay loyal to God in the tough times, you will know that your faith is real.

> Submit to God and be at peace with him;
> in this way prosperity will come to you.
>
> Job 22:21 (NIV)

January 10—Trust

There is a God in heaven who invites his children to hide under the shelter of his wings. God will never leave nor forsake you. Don't put your trust in anything other than life's absolutes, such as God's absolute faithfulness to those who put their trust in Him. God loves you and will protect you. That's what fathers do.

> Blessed is the man who makes the LORD his trust,
> who does not look to the proud, to those who turn aside to false gods.
>
> Psalms 40:4 (NIV)

January 11—Just Desserts

If everyone got what they deserved, who would be left? People do and say the wrong thing on a regular basis. Suppose you have an enemy and something bad happens to him. Why celebrate? Think about how many times you've escaped punishment after wronging someone. When you see the guilty punished, it should fill you with the fear of God. That punishment could have been yours.

> Do not gloat when your enemy falls; when he stumbles, do not let your heart rejoice, or the Lord will see and disapprove and turn his wrath away from him.
>
> Proverbs 24:17–18 (NIV)

January 12—Trials

Suffering leads to obedience, and obedience leads to blessings.

> In this you greatly rejoice, though now for a little while you may have had to suffer grief in all kinds of trials.
>
> 1 Peter 1:6 (NIV)

January 13—Hope

God is so good that he can take the worst possible circumstance and make something worthwhile come from it. Every impossible situation we struggle with is an opportunity to change and grow. And when we come out the other side victorious, it's a little bit easier to believe that God will always be there for us, time and time again.

> Not only so, but we also rejoice in our sufferings, because we know that suffering produces perseverance; perseverance, character; and character, hope. And hope does not disappoint us, because God has poured out his love into our hearts by the Holy Spirit, whom he has given us.
>
> Romans 5:3–5 (NIV)

January 14—God's Goodness

No matter how uncomfortable we are when stepping out in faith to do something the Lord has placed on our heart, we can do it without fear. Fear has to do with anxiety over potential failure. But with God by your side, failure is not an option. If the Lord is with you, then who can be against you? You may face opposition when following the will of God, but that is nothing compared to the reward that awaits the faithful!

> After this, the word of the LORD came to Abram in a vision: "Do not be afraid, Abram. I am your shield, your very great reward."
>
> Genesis 15:1 (NIV)

January 15—Seize the Day

Tomorrow isn't guaranteed; today could be your last. All you have is now: this moment. Make use of it to the best of your ability. Don't waste it by worrying about tomorrow.

> Therefore do not worry about tomorrow, for tomorrow will worry about itself. Each day has enough trouble of its own.
>
> Matthew 6:34 (NIV)

January 16—Freedom

God is the freest being in all creation. Anything the Lord wants to do he does with an infinite effect. But God is good. The Lord never does anything that is evil, for immorality is not in his nature. He is holy. Man was made to be like God (Genesis 1:26). Therefore, the truth is that man should be free from every form of bondage and slavery. God wants you well spiritually, financially, mentally, physically, and every other way imaginable. God wants us dependent on nothing in the universe other than himself. And being totally dependent on God will set us free from worry.

> Then you will know the truth, and the truth will set you free.
>
> John 8:32 (NIV)

January 17—Simplicity

When God is pleased with us, most everything goes right. There is no doubt that when we are in the will of God that we will be satisfied. Therefore, even if it seems strenuous to do what you know you should do, do it with a positive outlook, knowing that a great reward is on its way.

> And if we are careful to obey all this law before the Lord our God, as he has commanded us, that will be our righteousness.
>
> Deuteronomy 6:25 (NIV)

January 18—Goodness

This world offers many enticements that are intended to pull people out of the will of God. The media focuses on the negative;. Sex sells, and being bad comes more naturally to many people than being good. With that in mind, it is important to focus on the things that are pure: the Word of God, family, and all things unpolluted by the darkness of sin.

> Finally, brothers, whatever is true, whatever is noble, whatever is right, whatever is pure, whatever is lovely, whatever is admirable—if anything is excellent or praiseworthy—think about such things. Whatever you have learned or received or heard from me, or seen in me—put it into practice. And the God of peace will be with you.
>
> Philippians 4:8–9 (NIV)

January 19—The Long Run

Esau was not stranded on a deserted island for forty days without food. Near as anyone can tell, he was simply hungry. There was food to be had if he cooked it for himself, but his lust for instant gratification was self-defeating. He sold his birthright for a bowl of soup and some bread.

> Then Jacob gave Esau some bread and some lentil stew. He ate and drank, and then got up and left. So Esau despised his birthright.
>
> Genesis 25:34 (NIV)

January 20—Some are Sicker than Others

By nature, as decedents of Adam and Eve after the fall from grace, we are sick and afflicted by a sinful nature. By the immaculate conception, Jesus was free from this disease and was the only "well" human being ever created. His point in the gospel below is that some people are more sinful than others, but all are sinful, and we are to be merciful to those who are sick with sin, not judgmental.

> On hearing this, Jesus said, "It is not the healthy who need a doctor, but the sick. But go and learn what this means: 'I desire mercy, not sacrifice.' For I have not come to call the righteous, but sinners."
>
> Matthew 9:12–13 (NIV)

January 21—Sadness

Solomon began his rule with such wonderful hopes for a victorious reign. He was the richest and wisest king on earth. But he fell away from God as he grew used to a lavish lifestyle, and there is no replacing God, no matter how extravagant the accommodations. When we try to replace God with pleasure, life loses its meaning.

> A man can do nothing better than to eat and drink and find satisfaction in his work. This too, I see, is from the hand of God, for without him, who can eat or find enjoyment? [26] To the man who pleases him, God gives wisdom, knowledge and happiness, but to the sinner he gives the task of gathering and storing up wealth to hand it over to the one who pleases God. This too is meaningless, a chasing after the wind.
>
> Ecclesiastes 2:24–26 (NIV)

January 22—Grace

If a person were to be honest with himself, he'd be free to admit that he has weaknesses. Knowing what those weaknesses are is more than half the battle. Our deficiencies of character, however small, are footholds for the devil. But Jesus said that he would make up for our character defects through the power of grace.

> But he said to me, "My grace is sufficient for you, for my power is made perfect in weakness." Therefore I will boast all the more gladly about my weaknesses, so that Christ's power may rest on me.
>
> 2 Corinthians 12:9 (NIV)

January 23—Reverential Fear

The best way to demonstrate a reverential fear of the Lord is by not sinning intentionally. God will still correct you if you sin by accident, but there is nothing but sorrow for the person who continues to sin on purpose, he can look forward to trouble.

> For I dreaded destruction from God, and for fear of his splendor I could not do such things.
>
> Job 31:23 (NIV)

January 24—Human Nature

While humanism teaches that people are intrinsically and by nature good beings, Jeremiah 17:9 says, "The human heart is most deceitful and desperately wicked. Who really knows how bad it is?" That doesn't mean that people are rotten to the core; it just means that we need a Savior in order to live a life worth living.

> Now while he was in Jerusalem at the Passover Feast, many people saw the miraculous signs he was doing and believed in his name. But Jesus would not entrust himself to them, for he knew all men. He did not need man's testimony about man, for he knew what was in a man.
>
> John 2:23–25 (NIV)

January 25—Morning Cheer

Relying upon God for deliverance from the darkness of night into the brightness of morning is the key to letting go of worry and dread. It's good to know that no matter how bad a day might be, the following day could bring peace and joy. One never knows what's next!

> For his anger lasts only a moment, but his favor lasts a lifetime; weeping may remain for a night, but rejoicing comes in the morning.
>
> Psalm 30:5 (NIV)

January 26—The Power of Prayer

When life becomes unmanageable it is usually due to an absence of prayer. Having a sound prayer life is key to remaining calm in times of distress. Knowing the Lord intimately will provide you with the strength to keep going when everything inside you wants to quit.

> Let us then approach the throne of grace with confidence, so that we may receive mercy and find grace to help us in our time of need.
>
> Hebrews 4:16 (NIV)

January 27—Ask and Ye Shall Receive

There were two men crucified next to Jesus. One man forgot his pride and asked Jesus for help, while the other man mocked Jesus. Neither man had anything to lose by proclaiming Jesus as king. They would both be dead that day, their reputations were already shot, and yet only one out of two men took out an eternal "life insurance" plan.

> Then he said, "Jesus, remember me when you come into your kingdom."
> Jesus answered him, "I tell you the truth, today you will be with me in paradise."
>
> Luke 23:42–43 (NIV)

January 28—Surpassing Dread

When trouble enters your life, relief is usually right behind it.

> An anxious heart weighs a man down, but a kind word cheers him up.
>
> Proverbs 12:25 (NIV)

January 29—Persecution

Jesus told his disciples that no servant is greater than his master. He told his disciples that if people persecuted him, that they too would be persecuted. But have hope! No matter what problems people try to cause, there is a great God who will make things work out for your overall benefit.

> Blessed are you when people insult you, persecute you, and falsely say all kinds of evil against you because of me.
>
> Matthew 5:11 (NIV)

January 30—You're Covered

All living things have a destiny, but what do all living

things have in common? First, God made them, and second, God will take good care of them. Therefore, put worry in its place.

> If that is how God clothes the grass of the field, which is here today and tomorrow is thrown into the fire, will he not much more clothe you, O you of little faith?
>
> Matthew 6:30 (NIV)

January 31—Complaining

It's tempting to complain when things are bad, but God controls the times and seasons. Solomon said that there is a time and place for everything under the heavens; unfortunately, that includes suffering and grief. Therefore, when you know that God has promised something, don't make things worse by being negative toward God, who is capable of helping you, as that will only delay your breakthrough further.

> But the people were thirsty for water there, and they grumbled against Moses. They said, "Why did you bring us up out of Egypt to make us and our children and livestock die of thirst?"
>
> Exodus 17:3 (NIV)

February

February 1—Perspective

So much of life lies in our perspective. Everything is outlook. This means that you are capable of creating your own sense of reality based on the thoughts you generate. That is why the devil uses psychological warfare on humans since before their birth. He doesn't want you to know how great you are capable of becoming. You have more power in your faith than you could possibly imagine.

> Be careful how you think; your life is shaped by your thoughts.
>
> Proverbs 4:23 (GNT)

February 2—Love

Love is usually associated with a warm and fuzzy feeling. When you choose love, you are choosing to treat people the right way. After you make that decision, God will give you the power to be loving, and that is the truest sense of goodness.

> Love is patient, love is kind. It does not envy, it does not boast, it is not proud. It is not rude, it is not self-seeking, it is not easily angered, it keeps no record of wrongs. Love does not delight in evil but rejoices with the truth. It always protects, always trusts, always hopes, always perseveres. Love never fails.
>
> 1 Corinthians 13:4–8 (NIV)

February 3—The Key Is Balance

When life is good, it seems like life will be pleasant forever. But when disaster strikes, it seems like life will never look up again. But a brighter day is on its way. The key to successful living lies in not allowing life's ups to get you overly excited and not allowing life's lows to get you too discouraged. Life is a balancing act; therefore find your center and keep it.

> What strength do I have, that I should still hope? What prospects, that I should be patient?
>
> Job 6:11 (NIV)

February 4—Safe and Secure

Jesus knows what it feels like to be sad, joyful, angry, and even fearful. But he never felt the impact of failure. He is the ultimate champion of the people, and he wants to help you right now. No matter what you've done, good or bad, Jesus wants to love and strengthen you.

> The Lord is close to the brokenhearted and saves those who are crushed in spirit. A righteous man may have many troubles, but the Lord delivers him from them all.
>
> Psalm 34:18–19 (NIV)

February 5—Faith

It doesn't matter how right you are if the other person is too stubborn to admit that they were wrong. Even Jesus could not convince certain towns that he was sent by God to help the hurting. It is our useless pride that keeps us out of the will of God and consequently away from the victory that only God can give.

> Jesus said to them, "Only in his hometown, among his relatives and in his own house is a prophet without honor." He could not do any miracles there, except lay his hands on a few sick people and heal them. And he was amazed at their lack of faith.
>
> Mark 6:4–6 (NIV)

February 6—The End of the Road

Often the end of a season seems like the end of everything. This is especially true when it is the involuntary end of something in which you had placed a great amount of faith. But have hope! We serve an eternal God who loves and cares for us. The Lord is in control of the seasons of life and will carry you through to the starting line of another great adventure. Never give up.

> I will not die but live, and will proclaim what the Lord has done.
>
> Psalm 118:17 (NIV)

February 7—Equality

God is fair; everyone will be held responsible for their thoughts and desires. No man ever makes a fool of God. But God allows his children to make mistakes and learn from them. Suffering is the most effective teaching tool. Sometimes it takes an awful and painful catastrophe for a person to change his ways. And when there has been no wrong done and you suffer unjustly, have faith in God. He may have allowed suffering to take place in your life to keep you free from a temptation he saw coming your way.

> Let the Lord judge the peoples. Judge me, O Lord, according to my righteousness, according to my integrity, O Most High.
> O righteous God, who searches minds and hearts, bring to an end the violence of the wicked and make the righteous secure.
>
> Psalm 7:8–9 (NIV)

February 8—Tenacity

If you live a good and purposeful life, God will be pleased with you and show you favor. Believers can learn from the salmon, which always swim upstream against the mighty current to get to higher ground so that their destiny will be fulfilled. We swim against a strong and mighty current that leads into a bottomless abyss. It may not always be easy to live a good life, but the rewards of doing so far outweigh the pains caused by living righteously in a sinful world.

> The Lord saw how great man's wickedness on the earth had become, and that every inclination of the thoughts of his heart was only evil all the time. The Lord was grieved that he had made man on the earth, and his heart was filled with pain. So the Lord said, "I will wipe mankind, whom I have created, from the face of the earth—men and animals, and creatures that move along the ground, and birds of the air—for I am grieved that I have made them." But Noah found favor in the eyes of the Lord.
>
> Genesis 6:5–8 (NIV)

February 9—Redemption

After the flood, God made a promise to never destroy mankind again. He knew that his humans would let him down, but he had a son whom he was preparing to send into the world in order to create a way for those who wanted salvation to receive it.

> The Lord smelled the pleasing aroma and said in his heart: "Never again will I curse the ground because of man, even though every inclination of his heart is evil from childhood. And never again will I destroy all living creatures, as I have done."
>
> Genesis 8:21 (NIV)

February 10—Cleansed

Knowing what food is good for the body and what foods are toxic is the cornerstone of a healthy diet. And knowing right from wrong is the starting point of a wholesome life. Choose wisely. Your life depends on your decisions.

> Since we have these promises, dear friends, let us purify ourselves from everything that contaminates body and spirit, perfecting holiness out of reverence for God.
>
> 2 Corinthians 7:1 (NIV)

February 11—Gratefulness

The times God corrects you are opportunities to bond with the Holy Spirit. It's wonderful to have the magnitude of our sins explained to us by God so that we do not make that same mistake twice. How special it is to have a relationship with the Lord!

> Moreover, we have all had human fathers who disciplined us and we respected them for it. How much more should we submit to the Father of our spirits and live! Our fathers disciplined us for a

little while as they thought best; but God disciplines us for our good, that we may share in his holiness.

Hebrews 12:9–10 (NIV)

February 12—What is Better?

What would you prefer, wisdom and temporary poverty, or to be a fool with a large bank account? Wisdom is better because the wise will find a way of getting wealth and keeping it, whereas the foolish will squander whatever wealth he has.

> With me [wisdom] are riches and honor, enduring wealth and prosperity.
>
> Proverbs 8:18 (NIV)

February 13—Integrity

Honesty in action makes for a genuinely safe life; whereas dishonesty will lead the crooked into a trap that they themselves have set.

> The integrity of the upright guides them, but the unfaithful are destroyed by their duplicity.
>
> Proverbs 11:3 (NIV)

February 14—Taking God for Granted

We can be in God's presence for so long that we begin to feel like fish in water—no longer perceiving His greatness and neglecting his provision. This was true of the disciples when they couldn't understand the power of the feeding of the five thousand men.

> For they had not understood about the loaves; their hearts were hardened.
>
> Mark 6:52 (NIV)

February 15—Blindness

Every miracle in the gospel occurred on two levels: literal and symbolic. When Jesus literally healed a man who was born blind, he fixed the man's eyes. Whereas symbolically, Jesus was showing mankind that he takes away our hardness of heart, which makes a person spiritually blind, when we turn our lives over to his care and accept him as Lord. To be spiritually blind is to be unaware of God's life-giving presence in our everyday lives.

> He has blinded their eyes and deadened their hearts, so they can neither see with their eyes, nor understand with their hearts, nor turn—and I would heal them.
>
> John 12:40 (NIV)

February 16—Guidance

When we turn our lives over to the care of the Holy Spirit, it is for our own good. God calls his children sheep, who are helpless without a shepherd. Jesus is our Shepherd. When we put our faith in him, the Lord will give us supernatural understanding that gives us insight into all things relevant to our lives. Then you will know what to do in adverse circumstances.

> Trust in the LORD with all your heart and lean not on your own understanding; in all your ways acknowledge him, and he will make your paths straight.
>
> Proverbs 3:5–6 (NIV)

February 17—Choice

Suppose you were to stand at a fork in the road, and there was a sign that labeled the left fork "life" and the right fork "death." Only a fool would choose death. But the Bible tells us that the wages of sin is death, which makes a person wonder why people sin. It's probably due to the fact that the road to life leads to a higher elevation and requires more effort than the road to death, which is all downhill.

> To those who by persistence in doing good seek glory, honor and immortality, he will give eternal life. But for those who are self-seeking and who reject the truth and follow evil, there will be wrath and anger.
>
> Romans 2:7–8 (NIV)

February 18—God's Kingdom

When we do right, we are given peace by God; when we have peace, it leads to happiness and joy. The Bible tells us that the kingdom of God is not meat and drink but righteousness, peace, and joy. The joy we have gives us the strength to do the work God wants us to do. And when we do God's work, he will reward us with all the things that we desire.

> But seek first his kingdom and his righteousness, and all these things will be given to you as well.
>
> Matthew 6:33 (NIV)

February 19—Reverence

Solomon said that reverence for the Lord is the starting place for all knowledge and understanding. God is all things; no one can know everything about God, but we can continue learning from him for an eternity. The greatest gift he can give to his children is his own special wisdom. Respect for God is the cornerstone of a blessed life.

> The LORD is exalted, for he dwells on high;
> he will fill Zion with justice and righteousness.
> He will be the sure foundation for your times, a rich store of salvation and wisdom and knowledge;
> the fear of the LORD is the key to this treasure.
>
> Isaiah 33:5–6 (NIV)

February 20—Living Right

When you do the right thing in the face of adversity, God will pour blessings into your life. After the trial, you will have unsurpassable peace, joy, and hope. Put God first, and he will put you first.

> But seek first his kingdom and his righteousness, and all these things will be given to you as well.
>
> Matthew 6:33 (NIV)

February 21—A Jealous Love

God loves his children as a husband loves his bride. The Bible calls Christ the Bridegroom and the church his bride. In several places in the Old Testament, God accuses his people of acting like unfaithful wives. When you put the pleasures of this world ahead of a relationship with the Lord, he is going to make you aware of his feelings, perhaps unpleasantly.

> Be careful not to forget the covenant of the LORD your God that he made with you; do not make for yourselves an idol in the form of anything the LORD your God has forbidden. For the LORD your God is a consuming fire, a jealous God.
>
> Deuteronomy 4:23–24 (NIV)

February 22—Endurance

Opportunities for growth are often cloaked in unpleasant circumstances. But relax. Cheer up! The test can't last forever, and as long as your attitude stays as positive as you can keep it, the evil in this world will be forced to withdraw its attack. After the trial comes a resurrection of hope, joy, and satisfaction. Don't give up before the miracle occurs.

> Consider it pure joy, my brothers, whenever you face trials of many kinds, because you know that

the testing of your faith develops perseverance. Perseverance must finish its work so that you may be mature and complete, not lacking anything.

> James 1:2–4 (NIV)

February 23—Comfort

It is comforting to know that there is a God who wants to love us no matter how bad life gets. We can make a mess out of life, and God will restore us. People can cause us harm, and God will heal and bless us. Disaster can strike, and God will mend our tattered circumstances. We only need to ask, and his unconditional love will lead us back into the good life.

> The LORD is my rock, my fortress and my deliverer; my God is my rock, in whom I take refuge. He is my shield and the horn of my salvation, my stronghold.
>
> Psalm 18:2 (NIV)

February 24—Tough Times

Sometimes God allows the battles of life to get to the point of impossible before coming in and giving us the victory. But what we need to know is that God is trustworthy and he will never see us destroyed by the enemy.

> "Pharaoh will think, 'The Israelites are wandering around the land in confusion, hemmed in by the desert.' And I will harden Pharaoh's heart,

and he will pursue them. But I will gain glory for myself through Pharaoh and all his army, and the Egyptians will know that I am the LORD." So the Israelites did this.

Exodus 14:3–4 (NIV)

February 25—Slavery

Slavery is more of a mind-set than a status. The Israelites were free from Pharaoh and his whippings, but they were still captive to their own unbelief. What blinded them from seeing the possibilities of their new circumstances? What blinds us from seeing the possibilities of our circumstances? Maybe people are more focused on their obstacles than their potential.

> They said to Moses, "Was it because there were no graves in Egypt that you brought us to the desert to die? What have you done to us by bringing us out of Egypt? Didn't we say to you in Egypt, 'Leave us alone; let us serve the Egyptians'? It would have been better for us to serve the Egyptians than to die in the desert!"

Exodus 14:11–12 (NIV)

February 26—
The Battle Belongs to the Lord

God carries us through the circumstances he's not prepared us for yet. But the bottom line is that he wants his children to be ready for anything and afraid of nothing. There are some things in life that require a good fight on our part, but there are also times when we need to stop getting in God's way when he's trying to deliver us.

> Then the Lord's anger burned against Moses and he said, "What about your brother, Aaron the Levite? I know he can speak well. He is already on his way to meet you, and his heart will be glad when he sees you."
>
> Exodus 4:14 (NIV)

February 27—Tears Before Cheer

Often, trouble precedes prosperity. God doesn't give us perfect success without seeing us through hard times. If the Lord were to give us everything we wanted without paying our dues, then we wouldn't be as grateful as we ought to be.

> Remember how the Lord your God led you all the way in the desert these forty years, to humble you and to test you in order to know what was in your heart, whether or not you would keep his commands.
>
> Deuteronomy 8:2 (NIV)

February 28—His People

The righteous will suffer in this fallen world, but God will redeem them all when they wait upon Him.

> The LORD gives strength to his people; the LORD blesses his people with peace.
>
> Psalm 29:11 (NIV)

February 29—Welcome

There's no use staying where you're not welcome. Even Jesus had problems with people who refused to let him help them with their problems. Jesus said that no servant is better than his master, which means that his people will run into some of the same problems he ran into. In that case, do what he did, and go to another town.

> If the home is deserving, let your peace rest on it; if it is not, let your peace return to you.
>
> Matthew 10:13 (NIV)

March

March 1—Regular People

Moses found favor with God, not because of his status, but because God chose him. Life is random, and one never knows what God will choose to do next. You could be chosen today or the next day by the Almighty God to do something extraordinary. God is great, and he wants to do great things in your life. Just believe!

> But Moses said to God, "Who am I, that I should go to Pharaoh and bring the Israelites out of Egypt?"
>
> Exodus 3:11 (NIV)

March 2—All Things through Christ

After Moses declared his inadequacies before the Lord, God provided Moses with success's secret ingredient:

> And God said, "I will be with you. And this will be the sign to you that it is I who have sent you: When you have brought the people out of Egypt, you will worship God on this mountain."
>
> Exodus 3:12 (NIV)

March 3—Blessed

Nobody can be perfect, and in Jesus's Sermon on the Mount, his point is that the people who admit they can't be perfect are the ones that are going to receive the most help. Jesus did not come to help people who claim they don't need him. Everybody needs God's assistance because we all fall short of God's perfect standard.

> Blessed are the poor in spirit, for theirs is the kingdom of heaven.
>
> Matthew 5:3 (NIV)

March 4—Turn

Turning from our errors and shortcomings can often be a difficult and painful process. People develop habits that are hard to break. Whatever bad habits you might have, the Lord is standing by with the power to help you do away with your desire for what's wrong and to follow his perfect plan for your life.

> In those days John the Baptist came, preaching in the Desert of Judea and saying, "Repent, for the kingdom of heaven is near."
>
> Matthew 3:1–2 (NIV)

March 5—Reconciliation

The Bible is a love story. John 3:16 says, "For God so loved the world that he sent his only son." If you have ever had a fallout with someone you love and have gotten back together with them, then you know how wonderful it feels to be reconciled. God is calling all of his children who once were lost to again be found.

> We are therefore Christ's ambassadors, as though God were making his appeal through us. We implore you on Christ's behalf: Be reconciled to God.
>
> 2 Corinthians 5:20 (NIV)

March 6—Talents

Every time we take God up on an opportunity to use our talents to do good work for the kingdom of God, we open the doorway for more and more opportunities to do good for the kingdom of God. We will eventually open up the doors of unlimited blessings, swimming in heavenly rewards. If it is in your power to do good, do it; it's well worth the effort.

> When he returned after having received the kingdom, he ordered these bond servants to whom he had given the money to be called to him, that he might know how much each one had made by buying and selling. The first one came before him, and he said, Lord, your mina has made ten [additional] minas. And he said to him, Well done, excellent bond servant! Because you have been faithful and trustworthy in a very little [thing],

you shall have authority over ten cities. The second one also came and said, Lord, your mina has made five more minas. And he said also to him, And you will take charge over five cities. Then another came and said, Lord, here is your mina, which I have kept laid up in a handkerchief. For I was [constantly] afraid of you, because you are a stern (hard, severe) man; you pick up what you did not lay down, and you reap what you did not sow. He said to the servant, I will judge and condemn you out of your own mouth, you wicked slave! You knew [did you] that I was a stern (hard, severe) man, picking up what I did not lay down, and reaping what I did not sow? Then why did you not put my money in a bank, so that on my return, I might have collected it with interest? And he said to the bystanders, Take the mina away from him and give it to him who has the ten minas. And they said to him, Lord, he has ten minas [already]! And [said Jesus,] I tell you that to everyone who gets and has will more be given, but from the man who does not get and does not have, even what he has will be taken away.

Luke 19:15–26 (AMP)

March 7—Rest

It is a good thing to take time apart from the hectic aspects of everyday life to be at ease. God not only allows people to come into his presence for rest; he encourages us to rest.

> There remains, then, a Sabbath-rest for the people of God; for anyone who enters God's rest also

rests from his own work, just as God did from his.

Hebrews 4:9–10 (NIV)

March 8—Prophesy

The word of the Lord is infallible. Whatever God says will happen is what is going to end up happening, with or without his people's cooperation. The Lord set the Hebrew captives free from the tyrannical rule of Pharaoh while they fought him every step of the way. It took them forty years to make an eleven-day trip in the desert. It is to our benefit to cooperate when we hear God tell us to do something; one way or another, it's going to get done.

> Moses reported this to the Israelites, but they did not listen to him because of their discouragement and cruel bondage.
>
> Exodus 6:9 (NIV)

March 9—Reason to Rejoice

The Bible tells us that we are nothing more than a puff of vapor in time. Our existence on earth is brief. But there is life after death, and those who have given their eternal fates over to Christ have real reason to rejoice because they will be citizens in heaven with all of the benefits that come from being sons and daughters of the Most High God.

> He replied, "I saw Satan fall like lightning from heaven. I have given you authority to trample on snakes and scorpions and to overcome all the power of the enemy; nothing will harm you. However, do not rejoice that the spirits submit to you, but rejoice that your names are written in heaven."
>
> Luke 10:18–20 (NIV)

March 10—Faith

Even if you have the smallest amount of faith, you can do anything you deem necessary. It's not a lack of faith that is keeping you from achieving your breakthrough; rather, it is your doubt over whether or not you'll succeed. Get rid of your doubts and unbelief, and you will see your greatest ambitions actualized.

> He replied, "If you have faith as small as a mustard seed, you can say to this mulberry tree, 'Be uprooted and planted in the sea,' and it will obey you."
>
> Luke 17:6 (NIV)

March 11—Wisdom

To fear what God can do to you is the starting place of wisdom. You will know what to do in difficult circumstances when you use God's laws as your barometer.

> The fear of the LORD is the beginning of wisdom; all who follow his precepts have good understanding. To him belongs eternal praise.
>
> Psalm 111:10 (NIV)

March 12—The Other Cheek

God does not want his children to be the world's punching bag. That's not the point of telling us to turn the other cheek. The point is to love our enemies in spite of the way they are treating us so that they will see God's love flowing through us, be ashamed of their actions, and repent.

> "You have heard that it was said, 'Eye for eye, and tooth for tooth.' But I tell you, Do not resist an evil person. If someone strikes you on the right cheek, turn to him the other also."
>
> Matthew 5:38–39 (NIV)

March 13—Good Deeds in Private

Every action you make has an equal and opposite reaction. When you give something to somebody secretly, God will pay you back publically, though not necessarily in the same form. But when you seek public recognition for your good deeds, then all the reward you'll receive is a pat on the back.

> Be careful not to do your "acts of righteousness" before men, to be seen by them. If you do, you will have no reward from your Father in heaven.
>
> Matthew 6:1 (NIV)

March 14—Action Speaks Louder

There are two types of people: those who talk about doing the right thing and those who actually follow through on their promises. Proverbs tells us that there are many who claim to be trustworthy and true but just try to find somebody who truly is. Make a choice today to be the kind of person who follows through.

> Dear children, let us not love with words or tongue but with actions and in truth.
>
> 1 John 3:18 (NIV)

March 15—The Meaning of Life

The meaning of life comes down to loving God. And you can do that by spending time with him in prayer, meditating on his Word, and being loving to all people.

> "Teacher, which is the greatest commandment in the Law?" Jesus replied: "Love the Lord your God with all your heart and with all your soul and with all your mind.' This is the first and greatest commandment. And the second is like it: 'Love your neighbor as yourself.' All the Law and the Prophets hang on these two commandments."
>
> Matthew 22:36–40 (NIV)

March 16—Love

We serve a God that is perfect, a God who loves and is willing to forgive us our trespasses when we humbly repent. Christians need to be mindful of their actions, always asking the Lord to guide them, being sensitive to his promptings and discipline. The two most important pursuits are loving God and loving people. This is our call.

> As a prisoner for the Lord, then, I urge you to live a life worthy of the calling you have received. Be completely humble and gentle; be patient, bearing with one another in love.
>
> Ephesians 4:1–2 (NIV)

March 17—The Role of the Church

Jesus did a lot. But one major element to his legacy was the community he set up whose entire function was to serve one another out of love.

> It was he who gave some to be apostles, some to be prophets, some to be evangelists, and some to be pastors and teachers, to prepare God's people for works of service, so that the body of Christ may be built up until we all reach unity in the faith and in the knowledge of the Son of God and become mature, attaining to the whole measure of the fullness of Christ.
>
> Ephesians 4:11–13 (NIV)

March 18—Renewed Strength

We all want the ability to get through the day with power to spare. We all have the desire to do what we love and as a result be energized by our work, rather than drained by it. But in all tasks, remember that Jesus Christ is your boss. He will renew your energy to do the work he has given you the talent to do.

> But those who hope in the LORD will renew their strength. They will soar on wings like eagles; they will run and not grow weary, they will walk and not be faint.
>
> Isaiah 40:31 (NIV)

March 19—Patience

Impatience gets people in a great deal of unnecessary trouble. People often do and say things that they later regret and can't take back. Do yourself a favor by being patient. You don't have to like everything that happens to you, but it helps to have a patient approach.

> Better a patient man than a warrior, a man who controls his temper than one who takes a city.
>
> Proverbs 16:32 (NIV)

March 20—The Word's Purpose

People need their wrong behavior and mistakes explained to them so that the truth may be understood. Without knowing our errors, we won't repent, and without repentance, we won't progress. The Word of God convicts us of our sins and gives us the opportunity to make U-turns in life.

> All Scripture is God-breathed and is useful for teaching, rebuking, correcting and training in righteousness, so that the man of God may be thoroughly equipped for every good work.
>
> 2 Timothy 3: 16–17 (NIV)

March 21—Rejuvenation

The best feeling in the world comes from being guilt free. If you have a guilty conscience, you'll never be effective.

> Create in me a pure heart, O God, and renew a steadfast spirit within me.
>
> Psalm 51:10 (NIV)

March 22—Purpose

Your purpose is to do every task for which you are responsible to the best of your ability and to make progress every day. Adore God by treating his people with the dignity and respect they inherently deserve. Then you will show that you are reverent, and people will see you as being a shining light in dark places.

> And now, O Israel, what does the LORD your God ask of you but to fear the LORD your God, to walk in all his ways, to love him, to serve the LORD your God with all your heart and with all your soul, and to observe the LORD's commands and decrees that I am giving you today for your own good?
>
> Deuteronomy 10:12–13 (NIV)

March 23—Just Believe

Believers become miraculous achievers once they rid themselves of doubt, which is really fear, and become what they are meant to be: sons and daughters of the Most High.

> Jesus replied, "I tell you the truth, if you have faith and do not doubt, not only can you do what was done to the fig tree, but also you can say to this mountain, 'Go, throw yourself into the sea,' and it will be done."
>
> Matthew 21:21 (NIV)

March 24—Obedience

There is no escaping the omnipresent Almighty God of creation. Therefore, when a person knows that he is supposed to do something for God, he is just fooling himself if he thinks that he's going to get out of it by running away.

> The word of the LORD came to Jonah son of Amittai: "Go to the great city of Nineveh and preach against it, because its wickedness has come up before me." But Jonah ran away from the LORD and headed for Tarshish. He went down to Joppa, where he found a ship bound for that port. After paying the fare, he went aboard and sailed for Tarshish to flee from the LORD.
>
> Jonah 1:1–2 (NIV)

March 25—Safety in Jesus

Jesus is still in the miracle business. Today, perhaps more than any other time in history, God's divine intervention protects his people from disaster.

> Have no fear of sudden disaster or of the ruin that overtakes the wicked, for the LORD will be your

confidence and will keep your foot from being snared.

Proverbs 3:25–26 (NIV)

March 26—Nothing to Fear

Never allow the troubles of the world to make you abandon your faith.

> Shadrach, Meshach and Abednego replied to the king, "O Nebuchadnezzar, we do not need to defend ourselves before you in this matter. If we are thrown into the blazing furnace, the God we serve is able to save us from it, and he will rescue us from your hand, O king. But even if he does not, we want you to know, O king, that we will not serve your gods or worship the image of gold you have set up."

Daniel 3:16–18 (NIV)

March 27—Monotheism

Family and friends are essential, money is important, and a good career is key to survival. But nothing is greater than God; put nothing ahead of the Lord.

> This is what the Lord says—Israel's King and Redeemer, the Lord Almighty: I am the first and I am the last; apart from me there is no God.

Isaiah 44:6 (NIV)

March 28—Unbreakable Ties

From life through death and into the realm of eternity, God loves mankind with an impartial love that surpasses understanding. Then why are the two eternal fates—heaven and hell—so opposite in nature? The answer lies in the choice we are given between adapting to Christ's ways versus doing things our way. Following Christ leads to life everlasting while man's way leads to damnation. But no matter what you choose, God will always love you.

> Neither height nor depth, nor anything else in all creation, will be able to separate us from the love of God that is in Christ Jesus our Lord.
>
> Romans 8:39 (NIV)

March 29—The Cost

If you want to be like God, you must submit yourself to the needs of others. Be sensitive and do all you can to help those in need with your service and knowledge.

> Though I am free and belong to no man, I make myself a slave to everyone, to win as many as possible. To the weak I became weak, to win the weak. I have become all things to all men so that by all possible means I might save some.
>
> 1 Corinthians 9:19, 22 (NIV)

March 30—Rewards

Our God is a huge God who cares greatly about little things and rewards those with great riches for being faithful in small dealings.

> I tell you the truth, anyone who gives you a cup of water in my name because you belong to Christ will certainly not lose his reward.
>
> Mark 9:41 (NIV)

March 31—No Man Is an Island

Everything we do has a powerful effect on masses of people, and we are mostly unaware of this. This is shown to be true in several passages of scripture. The Bible says many times that we are the body of Christ, with Christ as our head. After all, one hand washes the other. Have you ever tried to wash one hand by itself? People need you.

> Do you help God by being so righteous? There is nothing God needs from you. It is your fellow man who suffers from your sins, and the good you do helps him.
>
> Job 35:7–8 (GNT)

April

April 1—Wait and See

Does it feel as if your prayers are falling on deaf ears in heaven? No, indeed, your prayers will receive an answer in God's perfect timing. Remember how God tempered Job's spirit during an entire season of inconceivable distress? But in the end of the book, God spoke in Job's favor.

> Job, you say you can't see God; but wait patiently—
> your case is before him.
>
> Job 35:14 (GNT)

April 2—Every Day Is a Gift

Human life is precious. Every day is a bonus day considering the fact that yesterday could have been your last. We have the privilege of starting over every day anew. Whatever mistakes made the day before can be erased by a decision to learn from our errors. By not sinning intentionally and refusing to compromise integrity, you will receive a blessing from God. That blessing starts with a pure conscience, and promises to end in a place that our wildest imaginations cannot even imagine.

> He who has clean hands and a pure heart, who does not lift up his soul to an idol or swear by what is false.
> He will receive blessing from the Lord and vindication from God his Savior.
>
> Psalms 24:4–5 (NIV)

April 3—Trust

There is always a reason to feel bad if you look for it. Thankfully, the opposite is just as true; there is always a reason to rejoice. Knowing that God is our protector gives us confidence in trying times.

> We wait in hope for the Lord; he is our help and our shield.
> In him our hearts rejoice, for we trust in his holy name.
>
> Psalms 33:20–21 (NIV)

April 4—Faith

You can do anything to which you set your mind. After all, one only needs a mustard-seed-size amount of faith to move mountains. Therefore imagine what you will do once you remove the hindrances of doubt and unbelief. Just believe!

> "'If you can'?" said Jesus. "Everything is possible for him who believes."
>
> Mark 9:23 (NIV)

April 5—Christ's Offering

It is difficult to comprehend the fundamentals of faith. God and Christ were together at the creation of the universe. Long before man existed, God knew that Christ would sacrificially die for the transgressions of our kind. All we need to do is, through faith, believe this fact and live in paradise with God for eternity.

> God made him who had no sin to be sin for us, so that in him we might become the righteousness of God.
>
> 2 Corinthians 5:21 (NIV)

April 6—Our Responsibility

When you look at life, you may ask yourself what the purpose of life is. Some say it is to be happy, while others say life's purpose is to make a difference. Paul said life is given to mankind so that each person who has a strength can use that advantage to help someone else who is in need.

> We who are strong ought to bear with the failings of the weak and not to please ourselves. Each of us

should please his neighbor for his good, to build him up.

Romans 15:1–2 (NIV)

April 7—Good Defeats Evil

Bless those who curse you. It's not because they deserve your love; bless them because it is the Lord's wish. Jesus called Judas "friend" right before Judas left the last supper to betray him. Later that night, in the garden when Jesus was being arrested, he miraculously healed the high priest's slave who was helping in the arrest. And upon the cross, Jesus prayed for the people who were killing him saying, "Forgive them, Father, they know not what they do." Think about it. How do you react when somebody accidently cuts you off in traffic? Consider what Jesus would do.

> On the contrary: "If your enemy is hungry, feed him; if he is thirsty, give him something to drink. In doing this, you will heap burning coals on his head." Do not be overcome by evil, but overcome evil with good.
>
> Romans 12:20–21 (NIV)

April 8—Avoiding Sin

Since being reborn into a spiritual nature, we are entitled to all the benefits of God's kingdom. This includes right standing in God's sight, peace of mind, and unspeakable joy. But sinning takes away from our spiritual sensitivity and leads us away from the good things of God.

> But take up the weapons of the Lord Jesus Christ, and stop paying attention to your sinful nature and satisfying its desires.
>
> Romans 13:14 (NIV)

April 9—The Law

God gave the Law to the Israelites so that they would know their sins, turn to him, and repent. Jesus came to earth to be the only man who would not break one of the Ten Commandments and die in place of everyone who has broken even the smallest of God's Laws: past, present, and future.

> Do not think that I have come to abolish the Law or the Prophets; I have not come to abolish them but to fulfill them. I tell you the truth, until heaven and earth disappear, not the smallest letter, not the least stroke of a pen, will by any means disappear from the Law until everything is accomplished.
>
> Matthew 5:17–18 (NIV)

April 10—Sound Advice

We all live in a world that is passing. One day, we will pass and be faced with the truth that we are going to be held accountable for every willful action we chose. Do your best today and every day to have the least amount of explaining to do on Judgment Day.

> Flee the evil desires of youth, and pursue righteousness, faith, love and peace, along with those who call on the Lord out of a pure heart.
>
> 2 Timothy 2:22 (NIV)

April 11—Salvation

There is exceptional pleasure in knowing that you will live in eternal paradise with the Father of creation. Consequently, there is a phenomenal degree of fear in the anticipation of an eternity excluded from the love of God.

> Do not cast me from your presence or take your Holy Spirit from me.
> Restore to me the joy of your salvation and grant me a willing spirit, to sustain me.
>
> Psalms 51:11–12 (NIV)

April 12—Just Call

No matter how deeply afflicted you are by the trials and storms of this life, you have the right and privilege of calling on God to deliver you from trouble safely.

> And call upon me in the day of trouble; I will deliver you, and you will honor me.
>
> Psalms 50:15 (NIV)

April 13—Words

God uses good people to bless others with their words. While the enemy uses the people whom he has hurt to hurt others with words in the form of lies, half-truths, and slander. Words are truly a double-edged sword. Therefore, think carefully before speaking. Your words carry great weight.

> They do not speak peaceably, but devise false accusations against those who live quietly in the land.
>
> Psalms 35:20 (NIV)

April 14—The Instruction Manual

Have you ever heard someone say that life doesn't come with instructions? That couldn't be a larger inaccuracy—the people of this earth have the Bible. Imagine living life without the comfort of being able to read and interact with God's Word on a daily basis.

> For everything that was written in the past was written to teach us, so that through endurance and the encouragement of the Scriptures we might have hope.
>
> Romans 15:4 (NIV)

April 15—Taxes

A great American patriot once stated that the two things in life that one can definitely count on are taxes and death. As you pay for your right to be a citizen of

America this year, count your blessings as you pay your dues. And remember, Jesus paid taxes too.

> "Then the sons are exempt," Jesus said to him. "But so that we may not offend them, go to the lake and throw out your line. Take the first fish you catch; open its mouth and you will find a four-drachma coin. Take it and give it to them for my tax and yours."
>
> Matthew 17:27 (NIV)

April 16—Equality

In God's sight, all of us are equal; whatever your talent, stay humble, because your talent is a gift from God. If you come across someone who claims to be holier than thou, just remember that no matter how impressive their gift is, as long as they act better than everyone else, they will lose their effectiveness due to their pride, and then where will they be?

> Do not let anyone who delights in false humility and the worship of angels disqualify you from the prize. Such a person goes into great detail about what he has seen, and his unspiritual mind puffs him up with idle notions. He has lost connection with the Head, from whom the whole body, supported and held together by its ligaments and sinews, grows as God causes it to grow.
>
> Colossians 2:18–19 (NIV)

April 17—Patience

From time to time, everyone, no matter how spiritually mature, will grow short with their fellow man. Even Jesus grew weary of dealing with the people's unbelief.

> "O unbelieving generation," Jesus replied, "how long shall I stay with you? How long shall I put up with you? Bring the boy to me."
>
> Mark 9:19 (NIV)

April 18—Values

Riches gained through dishonesty will eventually be as satisfying as sand in your mouth. But the little earned through honest ways is as satisfying as a good supper and a sound night's sleep.

> Better the little that the righteous have than the wealth of many wicked; for the power of the wicked will be broken, but the Lord upholds the righteous.
>
> Psalm 37:16–17 (NIV)

April 19—Tithing

Reverence for the Lord is like an all-access pass to the good things that God wants to give you. Tithe, and you show your trust and reverence for the Almighty.

> Be sure to set aside a tenth of all that your fields produce each year. Eat the tithe of your grain, new wine and oil, and the firstborn of your herds

and flocks in the presence of the LORD your God at the place he will choose as a dwelling for his Name, so that you may learn to revere the LORD your God always.

> Deuteronomy 14:22–23 (NIV)

April 20—Confess

No one can behave perfectly. We all fall short of God's glory; we all are subject to the ugliness of sin. We all need a Savior. Jesus is the Lord of heaven and earth. Anyone who confesses that truth will live forever in paradise with the King.

> That if you confess with your mouth, "Jesus is Lord," and believe in your heart that God raised him from the dead, you will be saved. For it is with your heart that you believe and are justified, and it is with your mouth that you confess and are saved.
>
> Romans 10:9–10 (NIV)

April 21—Chosen

The Bible tells us that many are called but few are chosen. This means that when we are called, it is our duty to make good choices through the guidance of the Holy Spirit. Then we will become holy over the course of time and will have more in common with God.

> Blessed are those you choose and bring near to live in your courts! We are filled with the good things of your house, of your holy temple.
>
> Psalms 65:4 (NIV)

April 22—Seek Ye First

When faithfulness to God is more important to you than pleasure, you will lead a worthwhile life. God doesn't promise that life will be easy, but living for God produces eternal benefits that begin in this life and resonate forever.

> Trust in the Lord and do good; dwell in the land and enjoy safe pasture.
> Delight yourself in the Lord and he will give you the desires of your heart.
>
> Psalms 37:3–4 (NIV)

April 23—Testing

God tests us for a reason. He already knows everything about us; therefore, his reason for testing us is so that we will succeed in learning about ourselves. If everyone is looting a city after a natural disaster, and you don't loot, God already knew that you wouldn't give into temptation. But now you know that you can stand up to temptation, and God's purpose is achieved.

> Remember how the Lord your God led you all the way in the desert these forty years, to humble you and to test you in order to know what was in your heart, whether or not you would keep his commands.
>
> Deuteronomy 8:2 (NIV)

April 24—Pay it Forward

God gives you the wisdom and experience to solve your problems. And when you see others in the same boat that you were once in, he likes to see you use that power to help others.

> Praise be to the God and Father of our Lord Jesus Christ, the Father of compassion and the God of all comfort, who comforts us in all our troubles, so that we can comfort those in any trouble with the comfort we ourselves have received from God.
>
> 2 Corinthians 1:3–4 (NIV)

April 25—Protection

When you let go of worries and put your hope in God, you will be guided by honesty, integrity, and character. Those characteristics protect a person.

> May integrity and uprightness protect me, because my hope is in you.
>
> Psalm 25:21 (NIV)

April 26—Dwell with the Lord

After giving your life over to the care of Jesus, it is important to spend time with him on a daily basis. You can do this in prayer, reading Christian literature, or just sitting in your garden.

> So then, just as you received Christ Jesus as Lord, continue to live in him, rooted and built up in

him, strengthened in the faith as you were taught, and overflowing with thankfulness.

> Colossians 2:6–7 (NIV)

April 27—Canceled Debt

What Christ did for you on the cross was better than having a one-trillion-dollar debt canceled, and one trillion dollars handed to you to spend as you wish.

> When you were dead in your sins and in the uncircumcision of your sinful nature, God made you alive with Christ. He forgave us all our sins, having canceled the written code, with its regulations, that was against us and that stood opposed to us; he took it away, nailing it to the cross.
>
> Colossians 2:13–14 (NIV)

April 28—Overly Attached

You don't have to sacrifice all earthly wealth to be of use to God, but be prepared to give away anything God asks you to give. Otherwise your possessions end up owning you.

> Jesus answered, "If you want to be perfect, go, sell your possessions and give to the poor, and you will have treasure in heaven. Then come, follow me."
>
> Matthew 19:21 (NIV)

April 29—Necessary Suffering

The reason Jesus was forced to suffer is because there are some things in life one will never succeed in learning about until they know what it feels like to suffer. Jesus is a high priest who understands all of our inadequacies because he suffered the consequences of all our sins on the cross at Calvary.

> During the days of Jesus' life on earth, he offered up prayers and petitions with loud cries and tears to the one who could save him from death, and he was heard because of his reverent submission. Although he was a son, he learned obedience from what he suffered
>
> Hebrews 5:7–8 (NIV)

April 30—God's Approval

When God is pleased with you, your life will go smoothly; even the bumps will seem less bumpy.

> And if we are careful to obey all this law before the LORD our God, as he has commanded us, that will be our righteousness.
>
> Deuteronomy 6:25 (NIV)

May

May 1—God Protects

As long as you have given your mind over to the care of the will of God, there is very little that will cause you real upset. Those whose faith is real will be able to accept life's inconsistencies, knowing that God is consistently loving, even when our circumstances are full of havoc.

> And the peace of God, which transcends all understanding, will guard your hearts and your minds in Christ Jesus.
>
> Philippians 4:7 (NIV)

May 2—Salvation

The urgency of getting to heaven is unsettling when you are uncertain whether you are going to get there. And while no one can earn salvation by being good, righteousness and good deeds are signs that you have already been saved.

> Watch out for false prophets. They come to you in sheep's clothing, but inwardly they are ferocious wolves. By their fruit you will recognize them. Do people pick grapes from thorn-bushes, or figs from thistles? Likewise every good tree bears good fruit, but a bad tree bears bad fruit. A good tree cannot bear bad fruit, and a bad tree cannot bear good fruit. Every tree that does not bear good fruit is cut down and thrown into the fire. Thus, by their fruit you will recognize them.
>
> Matthew 7:15–20 (NIV)

May 3—Favor

Everyone goes through dry spells. Job in the Old Testament most definitely did. But every night is followed by the warmth of the morning sun. You may be in a dry period, but take comfort; God will come to your aid.

> For he says, "In the time of my favor I heard you, and in the day of salvation I helped you." I tell you, now is the time of God's favor, now is the day of salvation.
>
> 2 Corinthians 6:2 (NIV)

May 4—Waiting on God

Patiently waiting on God for his blessings in trying times shows reverence for the Lord and brings us peace.

Waiting for God can be frustrating, however it helps to know that the Father knows best; the Lord is always working on our behalf behind the scenes. With that in mind, do all you can, accept the things you cannot change and pray for the courage to change the things you can. God will help you, just wait.

> Be still before the Lord and wait patiently for him; do not fret when men succeed in their ways, when they carry out their wicked schemes.
> Psalms 37:7 (NIV)

May 5—Worry and Anger

There's no point in worrying. The Bible tells us that worrying won't add a single day to a person's life. And anger is only one letter short of danger. Therefore, relax and cheer up—you'll live a longer healthier life.

> Refrain from anger and turn from wrath; do not fret—it leads only to evil.
> Psalm 37:8 (NIV)

May 6—Humility

There is a good reason for being humble—the Bible tells us that without God, we can do nothing.

> But the meek will inherit the land and enjoy great peace.
> Psalms 37:11 (NIV)

May 7—God's Lambs

We are God's Lambs in a world full of wolves. But don't worry if people try to cause you harm; Jesus said to bless those who persecute you because God is our Shepherd and we are protected by him.

> If you belonged to the world, it would love you as its own. As it is, you do not belong to the world, but I have chosen you out of the world. That is why the world hates you.
>
> John 15:19 (NIV)

May 8—Armor

The strongest defense we have against the powers of Satan is to keep doing right and refusing to do evil. Go to church often and read God's Word. Moreover, memorizing Scripture will keep your mind sharp against the devil's lies.

> Put on the full armor of God so that you can take your stand against the devil's schemes.
>
> Ephesians 6:11 (NIV)

May 9—Satisfaction

When you seek God's love in times of sorrow, there is always hope. Things might not turn out the way you expected, but they will end up just as good or better when God is in charge.

> O God, you are my God, earnestly I seek you; my soul thirsts for you, my body longs for you, in a dry and weary land where there is no water.
>
> Psalm 63:1 (NIV)

May 10—Forgiveness

It is vital to forgive someone who wrongs you, not for their sake as much as for your own. Being bitter hurts you more than anyone else.

> Bear with each other and forgive whatever grievances you may have against one another. Forgive as the Lord forgave you.
>
> Colossians 3:13 (NIV)

May 11—Sadness

There are two kinds of sadness: carnal sorrow and godly sorrow. Carnal sorrow comes from the punishment we bring on ourselves. Whereas godly sorrow is rooted in preventative medicine, used by God, to keep us away from danger.

> Yet now I am happy, not because you were made sorry, but because your sorrow led you to repentance. For you became sorrowful as God intended and so were not harmed in any way by us. Godly sorrow brings repentance that leads to salvation and leaves no regret, but worldly sorrow brings death.
>
> 2 Corinthians 7:9–10 (NIV)

May 12—Seeking Salvation

There are people who have visited heaven and/or hell upon a near-death experience. Books have been written about such supernatural encounters. One account showed a person touring hell with Jesus, and there was a section of hell where there were millions of people earnestly praying to God to forgive them for their sins. But it was too late.

> For what hope has the godless when he is cut off, when God takes away his life?
> Does God listen to his cry when distress comes upon him?
> Will he find delight in the Almighty? Will he call upon God at all times?
>
> Job 27:8–10 (NIV)

May 13—Reliance

People who rely solely on their own understanding to keep them out of trouble are in danger. We are called to live by faith, and part of that faith comes from knowing that we are not clever enough to make it through our lives without God's guidance.

> What he trusts in is fragile; what he relies on is a spider's web.
> He leans on his web, but it gives way; he clings to it, but it does not hold.
>
> Job 8:14–15 (NIV)

May 14—First Place

When you make God your top priority, everything else will fall into place—your loved ones will not be neglected.

> Anyone who loves his father or mother more than me is not worthy of me; anyone who loves his son or daughter more than me is not worthy of me.
>
> Matthew 10:37 (NIV)

May 15—Discovery

Finding Jesus allows a person to discover the truth about himself and the world in which he lives. Once you have been given the Holy Spirit and have surrendered your will over to the care of a loving God, you will start to see the secret truths of life. There is no limit to the things you will learn.

> My purpose is that they may be encouraged in heart and united in love, so that they may have the full riches of complete understanding, in order that they may know the mystery of God, namely, Christ, in whom are hidden all the treasures of wisdom and knowledge.
>
> Colossians 2:2–3 (NIV)

May 16—Worthwhile

Life can be unpleasant. But take into consideration the prizes that await those who diligently seek the Lord! If you only knew the wonderful things that were in store for you, you would be able to smile through your troubles while looking forward to a brighter day. Life's not easy, but it's well worth the trouble when you refuse to give up.

> Let us fix our eyes on Jesus, the author and perfecter of our faith, who for the joy set before him endured the cross, scorning its shame, and sat down at the right hand of the throne of God.
>
> Hebrews 12:2 (NIV)

May 17—It Starts at the Top

In the Old Testament, the lineage of kings is extensive. And the truth was that when the king did good, God was pleased, and the people were blessed. However, when the king worshiped idols and was immoral, God turned his back on the nation.

> When the righteous thrive, the people rejoice; when the wicked rule, the people groan.
>
> Proverbs 29:2 (NIV)

May 18—Adversity

God controls the times and the seasons. And even in times of adversity and great trouble, the King of the universe has his omnipotent hand lying gently on our lives with complete care for our welfare. King David must have felt that the Lord had forsaken him many times before God delivered him into the position of Israel's greatest king.

Into your hands I commit my spirit; redeem me, O Lord, the God of truth.

Psalm 31:5 (NIV)

May 19—Belief

Do you ever doubt the sun will rise? Then why do you doubt God's willingness to bring an end to your troubles? As long as there is life, there is hope. Stay hoping; God is to be trusted!

> The Lord said to Moses, "How long will these people treat me with contempt? How long will they refuse to believe in me, in spite of all the miraculous signs I have performed among them?"
>
> Numbers 14:11 (NIV)

May 20—Loneliness

It must have been a lonely moment for Jesus when he was in between two criminals on the cross being insulted by them as he died for their benefit. This is what the King endured for his people, and when you feel alone have courage, for Christ endured shame and horror for all who would be saved. Therefore, he knows how you feel.

> "Let this Christ, this King of Israel, come down now from the cross, that we may see and believe." Those crucified with him also heaped insults on him.
>
> Mark 15:32 (NIV)

May 21—Look Forward

At the end of the day when you lay your head down to rest, you may take comfort in knowing that at that moment, while you rest, Jesus is supervising the construction of your mansion in heaven.

> Do not let your hearts be troubled. Trust in God; trust also in me. In my Father's house are many rooms; if it were not so, I would not have told you. I am going there to prepare a place for you.
>
> John 14: 1–2 (NIV)

May 22—Victory

God is all present, all knowing, all powerful, and all loving. He is on your side and wants you to trust him with your life as you face today's challenges.

> He shall say: "Hear, O Israel, today you are going into battle against your enemies. Do not be fainthearted or afraid; do not be terrified or give way to panic before them. For the LORD your God is the one who goes with you to fight for you against your enemies to give you victory."
>
> Deuteronomy 20:3 (NIV)

May 23—Endurance

When you pursue a relationship with God, your energy and strength will be revitalized regularly, even in the toughest circumstances.

Therefore you do not lack any spiritual gift as you eagerly wait for our Lord Jesus Christ to be revealed. He will keep you strong to the end, so that you will be blameless on the day of our Lord Jesus Christ.

1 Corinthians 1:7–8 (NIV)

May 24—Obedience

Enjoying the work God has given you is more satisfying than savoring the fruits of your labor.

> Praise be to you, O Lord; teach me your decrees.
> With my lips I recount all the laws that come from your mouth.
> I rejoice in following your statutes as one rejoices in great riches.
>
> Psalms 119:12–14 (NIV)

May 25—Power

The Word of God is the power of goodness over evil. When you understand the significance of the stories in the Bible, your knowledge will give you peace of mind and victory.

> I write to you, fathers, because you have known him who is from the beginning. I write to you, young men, because you are strong, and the word of God lives in you, and you have overcome the evil one.
>
> 1 John 2:14 (NIV)

May 26—Security

Following Jesus is the best life insurance plan. By following him, you will endure trouble and hardship because no servant is above his master. Since Jesus was persecuted, you too will endure vexation and trials. But have courage. It's worth the struggle. The righteous man will be rewarded for his trouble, just as the wicked will suffer permanent disgrace. And when you have taken your last breath, He is with you to take you home to an eternal life free from worry in sunny and beautiful paradise.

> And this is the will of him who sent me, that I shall lose none of all that he has given me, but raise them up at the last day.
>
> John 6:39 (NIV)

May 27—Perfection

Christ was made perfect through his suffering. He suffered unbelievable agony but still did not sin in word or deed. Because he was a perfect man, God was able to use him to die sacrificially on behalf of all mankind.

> Although he was a son, he learned obedience from what he suffered and, once made perfect, he became the source of eternal salvation for all who obey him and was designated by God to be high priest in the order of Melchizedek.
>
> Hebrews 5: 9–10 (NIV)

May 28—Judging

The only true judge is the person who has been thoroughly tempted and still has not sinned. This person alone has the right to fairly assess a person's innocence or guilt.

> And he has given him authority to judge because he is the Son of Man. "Do not be amazed at this, for a time is coming when all who are in their graves will hear his voice and come out—those who have done good will rise to live, and those who have done evil will rise to be condemned."
>
> John 5:27–29 (NIV)

May 29—Finding God

When a person says that he doesn't believe in God, it is sort of like a fish saying he doesn't believe in water.

> For since the creation of the world God's invisible qualities—his eternal power and divine nature—have been clearly seen, being understood from what has been made, so that men are without excuse.
>
> Romans 1:20 (NIV)

May 30—Hidden Talents

When God gives you something, it is obviously valuable and meant to be invested. In the parable of the rich man who gave his servants gold, or "talents," Jesus was telling us to use our abilities to help each other and that only a wicked and self-centered person would keep God's gift all to himself.

> Then the man who had received the one talent came. "Master," he said, "I knew that you are a hard man, harvesting where you have not sown and gathering where you have not scattered seed. So I was afraid and went out and hid your talent in the ground. See, here is what belongs to you."
>
> His master replied, "You wicked, lazy servant! So you knew that I harvest where I have not sown and gather where I have not scattered seed? Well then, you should have put my money on deposit with the bankers, so that when I returned I would have received it back with interest.
>
> "Take the talent from him and give it to the one who has the ten talents. For everyone who has will be given more, and he will have an abundance. Whoever does not have, even what he has will be taken from him."
>
> Matthew 25:24–25 (NIV)

May 31—Deliverance

Even the most confusing and terrible circumstances will have happy endings when you seek the saving presence of God.

> The Lord said, "They are my people; they will not deceive me." And so he saved them from all their suffering. It was not an angel, but the Lord himself who saved them. In his love and compassion he rescued them.
>
> Isaiah 63:8–9 (GNT)

June

June 1—True Life

Through letting go of all things selfish, you will find your needs still getting met. Do for others, and God will do for you.

> For whoever wants to save his life will lose it, but whoever loses his life for me and for the gospel will save it.
>
> Mark 8:35 (NIV)

June 2—Government

The Bible tells us that all governments are in place by God's authorization. All governments have a role in carrying out God's plan on earth, whether they are fair or corrupt.

> Consequently, he who rebels against the authority is rebelling against what God has instituted, and those who do so will bring judgment on themselves. For rulers hold no terror for those who do right, but for those who do wrong. Do you want to be free from fear of the one in authority? Then do what is right and he will commend you.
>
> Romans 13: 2–3 (NIV)

June 3—The Eleventh Commandment

Pray for enough strength to be capable of treating people the way you want to be treated. It is sometimes a difficult commandment, but there is a good reason for it. If everybody obeyed this command, there would be no more war.

> Let no debt remain outstanding, except the continuing debt to love one another, for he who loves his fellowman has fulfilled the law. The commandments, "Do not commit adultery," "Do not murder," "Do not steal," "Do not covet," and whatever other commandment there may be, are summed up in this one rule: "Love your neighbor as yourself."
>
> Romans 13:8–9 (NIV)

June 4—Worth

Humans are made in God's image. That means that we have inherent worth and value. No matter what the world might have to say to the contrary, you are significant.

> When I consider your heavens, the work of your fingers, the moon and the stars, which you have set in place, what is man that you are mindful of him, the son of man that you care for him?
>
> Psalm 8:3–4 (NIV)

June 5—Pray

When you're tempted to criticize somebody, pray for them instead. It's the civil thing to do, and far more helpful.

> You, then, why do you judge your brother? Or why do you look down on your brother? For we will all stand before God's judgment seat.
>
> Romans 14:10 (NIV)

June 6—Gratitude

The most unpleasant thing a believer endures in life is not even comparable to the fate that awaits the evil people of this earth after death.

> In that day the Lord will punish the powers in the heavens above and the kings on the earth below. They will be herded together like prisoners bound in a dungeon; they will be shut up in prison and be punished after many days.
>
> Isaiah 24:21–22 (NIV)

June 7—A Horticulture Parable

A vine can live with every branch cut off, but no branch can support itself after it has been cut from the vine.

> I am the vine; you are the branches. If a man remains in me and I in him, he will bear much fruit; apart from me you can do nothing.
>
> John 15:5 (NIV)

June 8—Never Alone

At times it seems that we are all alone, that no one understands our trouble. But God, who understands all things, is surrounding you right now with his love and protection.

> But a time is coming, and has come, when you will be scattered, each to his own home. You will leave me all alone. Yet I am not alone, for my Father is with me.
>
> John 16:32 (NIV)

June 9—Safety

We live in a fallen world with a fallen angel running loose trying to make everybody in the human race rebel against God. And his reason for doing that is to keep us from knowing God and receiving the special victory he gives.

> My prayer is not that you take them out of the world but that you protect them from the evil one.
>
> John 17:15 (NIV)

June 10—Grace

Grace is the enablement we receive from God to go through difficult situations with great success. Supposing that you have a large assignment from God, as did the Apostle Paul, then you are likely to see certain hardships. The larger the dent a person makes in the world, the more the Enemy will come against them. Or, look at Dr. Martin Luther King Jr. who was a hero in the faith and did a great deal. He has a major street named after him in nearly every U.S. city. But he suffered greatly for his efforts and was martyred. Yet the work that he did has caused a chain reaction that is still at work today. King did his work in peace because God called him to do a big job. Undoubtedly he felt afraid when receiving death threats, but he was a peacemaker who knew who he was in Christ. And like Christ, King accepted God's grace to move the Civil Rights movement to where it is today. You can't earn grace; God gives it to his children when they need it.

> And if by grace, then it is no longer by works; if it were, grace would no longer be grace.
>
> Romans 11:6 (NIV)

June 11—Remove Regret

It's a wonderful thing to know and carry out the will of God. People who are aware of their destinies, and are actively pursuing their heart's desire, will be free from guilt and regret. The saddest thing is to reach an old age and reflect on all the things you should have done but didn't.

> So whatever you believe about these things keep between yourself and God. Blessed is the man who does not condemn himself by what he approves.
>
> Romans 14:22 (NIV)

June 12—Conscience

A person needs to have enough insight into his own conscience to know whether he should be doing something or not. If I were to watch something I knew was not in line with my moral compass, I would be convicted of sin. Since turning my life over to the Lord's guidance, there are many things I have given up. But I have gained so much more!

> But the man who has doubts is condemned if he eats, because his eating is not from faith; and everything that does not come from faith is sin.
>
> Romans 14:23 (NIV)

June 13—Pride

It is simple to remain humble when times are bad, but when God gives abundant prosperity, it is possible to become arrogant, believing that you did it all by yourself. God gave all of us our talents, and the will to use them; therefore, rejoice in God's gifts—just don't take credit for them.

> You, then, why do you judge your brother? Or why

do you look down on your brother? For we will all stand before God's judgment seat.

Romans 14:10 (NIV)

June 14—In Due Time

God is never late, he is on time every time. When your dream seems delayed, know that God is using the present time to equip you to handle all the responsibility that your breakthrough will come with.

> Now the LORD was gracious to Sarah as he had said, and the LORD did for Sarah what he had promised. Sarah became pregnant and bore a son to Abraham in his old age, at the very time God had promised him.
>
> Genesis 21:1–2

June 15—A God-Sent Bride

There is no such thing as a perfect mate, just the perfect mate for you. The longer I'm married, the luckier I feel. Never in my life have I been this in love. My wife is a good and wonderful partner who never fails to surprise me.

> A wife of noble character who can find? She is worth far more than rubies. Her husband has full confidence in her and lacks nothing of value. She brings him good, not harm, all the days of her life.
>
> Proverbs 31:10–12 (NIV)

June 16—Forgiveness

No matter what a person has done, Jesus can save him from his mistakes when he chooses to stop doing wrong, accept the Lord as his personal savior, and seek forgiveness.

> Seek the Lord while he may be found; call on him while he is near.
> Let the wicked forsake his way and the evil man his thoughts.
> Let him turn to the Lord, and he will have mercy on him, and to our God, for he will freely pardon.
>
> Isaiah 55:6–7 (NIV)

June 17—Spirit

We're not supposed to be afraid of the pitfalls that terrify others. Jesus has given us his personal peace, which surpasses our understanding to be effective, even in times of trouble.

> For God did not give us a spirit of timidity, but a spirit of power, of love and of self-discipline.
>
> 2 Timothy 1:7 (NIV)

June 18—Necessary Suffering

We would all love to get a guarantee that for the rest of our lives there would be no more suffering. However, suffering is a teaching tool used by God. It teaches us what not to do. And knowing what not to do is half the battle.

> Endure hardship with us like a good soldier of Christ Jesus.
>
> 2 Timothy 2:3 (NIV)

June 19—Understanding

To understand the complexity of the Bible is to have a map to the universe tattooed inside your mind. When you are born again with God's Holy Spirit living inside you, through study and time, you can know enough about life to be ready for anything.

> Reflect on what I am saying, for the Lord will give you insight into all this.
>
> 2 Timothy 2:7 (NIV)

June 20—Keep Keeping On

Keep going in the right direction, and you will eventually reign victorious.

> If we endure, we will also reign with him. If we disown him, he will also disown us;
>
> 2 Timothy 2:12 (NIV)

June 21—Love

The more experienced a person becomes, the more they discover the value of kindness. I am intrigued by the ministry of Jesus. He loved those who were hurling insults at him while he died for them on the cross by praying to God on their behalf. Now that's love.

> Now that you have purified yourselves by obeying the truth so that you have sincere love for your brothers, love one another deeply, from the heart.
>
> 1 Peter 1:22 (NIV)

June 22—Anger

Holding a grudge against someone can be just as dangerous as holding burning coals against your chest. Your personal anger can only do harm; therefore, look for a reason to forgive and make amends, even if you're in the right.

> "In your anger do not sin": Do not let the sun go down while you are still angry, and do not give the devil a foothold.
>
> Ephesians 4:26–27 (NIV)

June 23—Intercessor

Overcoming evil with good takes courage and great willpower, but if you withstand the pressures of evil, you could very well turn enemies into good friends.

> And the Lord's servant must not quarrel; instead, he must be kind to everyone, able to teach, not resentful. Those who oppose him he must gently instruct, in the hope that God will grant them

repentance leading them to a knowledge of the truth, and that they will come to their senses and escape from the trap of the devil, who has taken them captive to do his will.

2 Timothy 2:24–26 (NIV)

June 24—Living the Life

Life is a challenge to us all. The Bible tells us that the righteous man will be persecuted and the wicked will be lost. Our only hope is the salvation that Christ gives, and the mercy anew each morning.

In fact, everyone who wants to live a godly life in Christ Jesus will be persecuted, while evil men and impostors will go from bad to worse, deceiving and being deceived.

2 Timothy 3:12 (NIV)

June 25—The Human Race

Run your own race. Don't worry about what others are doing or not doing. Do what God commands you to do whether it is popular or not. In the end, your reward is determined by how many things you did in obedience to God to the best of your ability.

I have fought the good fight, I have finished the race, I have kept the faith.

2 Timothy 4:7 (NIV)

June 26—Power to Spare

God will get you where you need to go in life when you cooperate with him. And he won't stop until you're a finished product, perfect by all standards.

> being confident of this, that he who began a good work in you will carry it on to completion until the day of Christ Jesus.
>
> Philippians 1:6 (NIV)

June 27—God Gives Victory

Remain calm when facing trouble because you have already been declared victorious by the King of the Universe!

> Whatever happens, conduct yourselves in a manner worthy of the gospel of Christ. Then, whether I come and see you or only hear about you in my absence, I will know that you stand firm in one spirit, contending as one man for the faith of the gospel without being frightened in any way by those who oppose you. This is a sign to them that they will be destroyed, but that you will be saved—and that by God.
>
> Philippians 1:27–28 (NIV)

June 28—Looking Forward

Letting go gives us strength to go on. When we are overly concerned with where we've been, there is no room to examine the prospects of where we are.

> Brothers, I do not consider myself yet to have taken hold of it. But one thing I do: Forgetting what is behind and straining toward what is ahead,
>
> Philippians 3:13 (NIV)

June 29—This Age

This age is coming to a close. The worries and difficulties that we are preoccupied with, the worries and difficulties that prevent us from knowing the will of God, will soon be nothing but a memory. Hold on; our Lord is coming.

> Let your gentleness be evident to all. The Lord is near.
>
> Philippians 4:5 (NIV)

June 30—Contentment

Anybody can be happy when everything is going their way, but it takes a mature person to remain positive when life is uncomfortable.

> I know what it is to be in need, and I know what it is to have plenty. I have learned the secret of being content in any and every situation, whether well fed or hungry, whether living in plenty or in want.
>
> Philippians 4:12 (NIV)

July

July 1—Yes You Can

Most people are drawn toward dreams that are attainable. With God's help, you can do anything; however, you will have to do your part. God will do what you can't, but the rest is up to you.

> I can do everything through him who gives me strength.
>
> Philippians 4:13 (NIV)

July 2—Practice What You Preach

The Bible shows us that teachers will be judged by a more rigorous standard than anybody else. For that reason, it is vital that all people in positions of ministry show the world what it means to be a straight-arrow

Christian, one who does not deviate from the code of morals, ethics, and laws of the faith.

> When I saw that they were not acting in line with the truth of the gospel, I said to Peter in front of them all, "You are a Jew, yet you live like a Gentile and not like a Jew. How is it, then, that you force Gentiles to follow Jewish customs?"
>
> Galatians 2:14 (NIV)

July 3—Believe

Abraham, the father of many nations, received a promise from God. He simply believed God's promise and was consequently considered holy by the Lord. God is willing to do so much for those who believe. All he requires from his children is faith.

> So those who have faith are blessed along with Abraham, the man of faith.
>
> Galatians 3:9 (NIV)

July 4—Inheritance

Eternal life is an unending highway of good things, and life on earth is the onramp. You who have accepted Christ's sacrifice are entering the most blissful and satisfying experience in the universe. Be patient; slow and steady wins the race. In this life you will see people flying past you, but know that those who speed through life are often not going anywhere. Just be aware that you are God's child, and that things are not always what they seem.

So you are no longer a slave, but a son; and since you are a son, God has made you also an heir.

> Galatians 4:7 (NIV)

July 5—Resurfacing

Did you ever quit a bad habit and then years later feel tempted to pick it up again? Paul addresses this tendency in the Bible—if this sounds familiar, you are not alone.

> Formerly, when you did not know God, you were slaves to those who by nature are not gods. But now that you know God—or rather are known by God—how is it that you are turning back to those weak and miserable principles? Do you wish to be enslaved by them all over again?
>
> Galatians 4:8–9 (NIV)

July 6—Reaping and Sowing

Give love, get love. Be hateful, receive scorn.

> The entire law is summed up in a single command: "Love your neighbor as yourself." If you keep on biting and devouring each other, watch out or you will be destroyed by each other.
>
> Galatians 5:14–15 (NIV)

July 7—Spirituality versus Carnality

Pursue what is good and lovely, and you will be less

likely to sin. If you put yourself in tempting situations, you are likely to lust and succumb to temptation's lure.

> So I say, live by the Spirit, and you will not gratify the desires of the sinful nature.
>
> Galatians 5:16 (NIV)

July 8—Nature

Inside all men is a war between good and evil. A choice must be made to follow the direction of God's Holy Spirit while ignoring the lust of the flesh. By pursuing God's goodness, you will be more likely to live a long and pleasant life, earning treasure upon treasure in heaven.

> For the sinful nature desires what is contrary to the Spirit, and the Spirit what is contrary to the sinful nature. They are in conflict with each other, so that you do not do what you want. But if you are led by the Spirit, you are not under law.
>
> Galatians 5:17–18 (NIV)

July 9—Value

God will care for you. All you have to do is surrender your will and accept God's direction. When properly guided, you will accomplish great things. You are the apple of God's eye. He loves you and wants to see good things happen to you.

> Are not five sparrows sold for two pennies? Yet not one of them is forgotten by God. Indeed, the very hairs of your head are all numbered. Don't be afraid; you are worth more than many sparrows.
>
> Luke 12:6–7 (NIV)

July 10—Good Fruit

People who have the fruit of the Spirit working in their lives have peace in times of trouble, joy in times of sorrow, and clarity in the face of confusion. And all these fruits come from God's unconditional love stemming from the Holy Spirit.

> But the fruit of the Spirit is love, joy, peace, patience, kindness, goodness, faithfulness, gentleness and self-control. Against such things there is no law.
>
> Galatians 5:22–23 (NIV)

July 11—Conscience

You always know if you have tried your best, when you could have given more effort, and what area of your performance could use improvement. Don't go by anybody else's success or failure; at the end of the day, the only person you're responsible for is yourself.

> Each one should test his own actions. Then he can take pride in himself, without comparing himself to somebody else.
>
> Galatians 6:4 (NIV)

July 12—Reaping and Sowing

If you do good things, God will bless you. If you do bad things, God will curse you.

> Do not be deceived: God cannot be mocked. A man reaps what he sows.
>
> Galatians 6:7 (NIV)

July 13—Vigilance

When we continue to do the right thing, even when it is hard—especially when it is hard—our day of victory will surely come.

> Let us not become weary in doing good, for at the proper time we will reap a harvest if we do not give up. Therefore, as we have opportunity, let us do good to all people, especially to those who belong to the family of believers.
>
> Galatians 6:9–10 (NIV)

July 14—In Christ

God is no respecter of persons. From the billionaire to the homeless, everyone is equal in God's sight because Christ died for everyone.

> Here there is no Greek or Jew, circumcised or uncircumcised, barbarian, Scythian, slave or free, but Christ is all, and is in all.
>
> Colossians 3:11 (NIV)

July 15—Education

The best education a person can receive comes from within.

> As for you, the anointing you received from him remains in you, and you do not need anyone to teach you. But as his anointing teaches you about all things and as that anointing is real, not counterfeit—just as it has taught you, remain in him.
>
> 1 John 2:27 (NIV)

July 16—Conscience

Having a clean conscience helps you through difficult circumstances. Knowing that your case is before a just God, who favors the innocent, gives you the power to tolerate trials with confidence.

> Dear friends, if our hearts do not condemn us, we have confidence before God and receive from him anything we ask, because we obey his commands and do what pleases him.
>
> 1 John 3:21–22 (NIV)

July 17—Laws and Commands

God is all knowing. God is all loving. And God has a perfect plan for your life, a plan made specifically for you! Knowing those three things leads a person to one conclusion: we are to be obedient Christians; it is in our best interest.

> But the children rebelled against me: They did not follow my decrees, they were not careful to keep my laws—although the man who obeys them will live by them—and they desecrated my Sabbaths. So I said I would pour out my wrath on them and spend my anger against them in the desert.
>
> Ezekiel 20:21 (NIV)

July 18—Repentance

God is all love. When an evil person dies and meets doom, it makes God sad.

> Do I take any pleasure in the death of the wicked? declares the Sovereign Lord. Rather, am I not pleased when they turn from their ways and live?
>
> Ezekiel 18:23 (NIV)

July 19—The Ways of the Lord

Only through prayer and application of God's Word can a person achieve holiness. Holiness does not mean perfection. Holiness is the reward God gives to those who diligently seek him after they have been tested by fire and their faith has been proved true. It is in this state of holiness that a person may come to catch a glimpse of what the Lord does and succeed in learning about the ways of the Most High God. There is a small portion of people who come to achieve holiness. There is far more profit in the acquired talent of mortal holiness than there is in gold.

> "For my thoughts are not your thoughts, neither are your ways my ways," declares the Lord. "As the heavens are higher than the earth, so are my ways higher than your ways and my thoughts than your thoughts."
>
> Isaiah 55:8–9

July 20—Coverage

Goodness is the best defense against wickedness, and the best demonstration of goodness comes from loving your fellow man.

> Above all, love each other deeply, because love covers over a multitude of sins.
>
> 1 Peter 4:8 (NIV)

July 21—Sacrifice

God will probably not ask you to lay your life down for somebody else, but he may want you to put somebody else's needs in front of your own.

> This is how we know what love is: Jesus Christ laid down his life for us. And we ought to lay down our lives for our brothers.
>
> 1 John 3:16 (NIV)

July 22—Delight

Appreciate your wife. She has been sent to you by God. She is a symbol of God's love for you.

Husbands, love your wives and do not be harsh with them.

Colossians 3:19 (NIV)

July 23—Knowledge

To know what you are talking about is better than having a large bank account. Knowledge and truth are worth more than gold.

> To the discerning all of them are right; they are faultless to those who have knowledge.
> Choose my instruction instead of silver, knowledge rather than choice gold.

Proverbs 8:9–10 (NIV)

July 24—Human Nature

The only proper place for a person's faith is in God. No matter how good a person may be, he still has a human nature that will disappoint himself and others from time to time.

> But Jesus would not entrust himself to them, for he knew all men. He did not need man's testimony about man, for he knew what was in a man.

John 2:24–25 (NIV)

July 25—Priorities

All the gold in the world is not worth more than your soul. It is better to be poor with peace than to be wealthy and unsatisfied with who you have become.

> What good is it for a man to gain the whole world, yet forfeit his soul? Or what can a man give in exchange for his soul?
>
> Mark 8:36–37 (NIV)

July 26—Proof

Gentiles became believers in Christ because they willingly let go of their doubts, worries, and fears. They simply heard Jesus speak, recognized the truth of his words, and believed, which consequently changed their lives forever.

> They said to the woman, "We no longer believe just because of what you said; now we have heard for ourselves, and we know that this man really is the Savior of the world."
>
> John 4:42 (NIV)

July 27—Gospel

The words in the gospel of Christ will endure for eternity. They will save anyone who reads them and believes.

> I am not ashamed of the gospel, because it is the power of God for the salvation of everyone who believes: first for the Jew, then for the Gentile.
>
> Romans 1:16 (NIV)

July 28—Peace

Having a clean conscience gives a person peace. Knowing that God is pleased with your efforts in the faith is rewarding.

> Therefore, since we have been justified through faith, we have peace with God through our Lord Jesus Christ.
>
> Romans 5:1 (NIV)

July 29—No Longer

Satan needs people to sin. He relies on our disobedience to God for the advancement of his cause. He makes wrong look right; he's been slowly and craftily making society accept wrong in the place of right for generations. He may be a defeated foe, but he can rule over a person if they give him their power by sinning.

> For we know that our old self was crucified with him so that the body of sin might be done away with, that we should no longer be slaves to sin.
>
> Romans 6:6 (NIV)

July 30—A High Priest Who Understands

Having Jesus as your Lord and Savior is like having the best boss in the world. He completely understands our mistakes, and will never fire us! We would have to quit the faith first, and even if we did, Jesus is always willing to rehire. God is good.

> For we do not have a high priest who is unable to sympathize with our weaknesses, but we have one who has been tempted in every way, just as we are—yet was without sin. Let us then approach the throne of grace with confidence, so that we may receive mercy and find grace to help us in our time of need.
>
> Hebrews 4:15–16 (NIV)

July 31—Sensitivity

God demonstrated his compassion in the Old Testament time and again. And if God was merciful enough to spare sinners before the age of grace, how much more grace can we look forward to enjoying in these last days?

> But the LORD said, "You have been concerned about this vine, though you did not tend it or make it grow. It sprang up overnight and died overnight. But Nineveh has more than a hundred and twenty thousand people who cannot tell their right hand from their left, and many cattle as well. Should I not be concerned about that great city?"
>
> Jonah 4:10–11 (NIV)

August

August 1—Soul Armor

Guard yourself with the knowledge that tells you the difference between right and wrong. Then pray for the power to resist the pleasurable sins that take you out of the will of God and into danger's path.

> Put on the full armor of God so that you can take your stand against the devil's schemes.
>
> Ephesians 6:11 (NIV)

August 2—It's a Long Run

Life can be disappointing and discouraging Discouragement is a frustrating condition. Sometimes it seems like life will never be bright again. But after God's done with teaching you obedience through your suffering, he will remove the trouble and restore your soul.

Man born of woman is of few days and full of trouble.

Job 14:1 (NIV)

August 3—Attitude

An airplane weighs tons, and yet it soars higher than the strongest leanest eagle. As long as the upward thrust of the engine overpowers the downward pull of gravity, that plane will fly wherever the pilot wants it to go. Nothing will stand in its way. Having a faith-driven, positive, can-do attitude will give you the thrust needed to overcome any obstacle in your way.

> Your attitude should be the same as that of Christ Jesus: Who, being in very nature God, did not consider equality with God something to be grasped, but made himself nothing, taking the very nature of a servant, being made in human likeness.
>
> Philippians 2:5–7 (NIV)

August 4—Gratitude

Being thankful to God for all that he has given you can keep your heart strong when times are tough. If you run out of things to be thankful for, give thanks for life itself.

> It is good to praise the LORD and make music to your name, O Most High, to proclaim your love in the morning and your faithfulness at night.
>
> Psalms 92:1–2 (NIV)

August 5—A Servant's Heart

When feeling bad, a person generally wishes to be left alone. But it is interesting to notice that when you do something for somebody else, whatever was bothering you tends to disappear.

> Jesus called them together and said, "You know that those who are regarded as rulers of the Gentiles lord it over them, and their high officials exercise authority over them. Not so with you. Instead, whoever wants to become great among you must be your servant, and whoever wants to be first must be slave of all."
>
> Mark 10:42–44 (NIV)

August 6—A Reason to be Kind

As you go out into the world today, remember that through your kindness to others, God's own personality will shine through you, blessing you and all others concerned. A more loving world starts with you.

> But love your enemies, do good to them, and lend to them without expecting to get anything back. Then your reward will be great, and you will be sons of the Most High, because he is kind to the ungrateful and wicked.
>
> Luke 6:35 (NIV)

August 7—Believe

Jesus is willing and able to help anyone who asks for his assistance. He can do anything—he can help anyone. Just believe!

> Then Jesus said to the centurion, "Go! It will be done just as you believed it would." And his servant was healed at that very hour.
>
> Matthew 8:13 (NIV)

August 8—Original Sin

Before mankind lost the right to paradise on earth, God already had a plan in mind for our redemption. It took Adam one moment to get mankind cursed and Jesus an entire lifetime of suffering to lift the curse. The good news is that the curse is lifted!

> To Adam he said, "Because you listened to your wife and ate from the tree about which I commanded you, 'You must not eat of it,' "Cursed is the ground because of you; through painful toil you will eat of it all the days of your life."
>
> Genesis 3:17 (NIV)

August 9—Why Obedience?

Many people believe that God's difficult rules are too hard and that following them is a form of slavery. But God's high expectations are for our own benefit. We have to try extra hard to live up to God's standard, but when we try we will make progress every day. And one day, we will have climbed a mountain and have much to be proud of.

> See, I set before you today life and prosperity, death and destruction. For I command you today to love the Lord your God, to walk in his ways, and to keep his commands, decrees and laws; then you will live and increase, and the Lord your God will bless you in the land you are entering to possess.
>
> Deuteronomy 30:15–16 (NIV)

August 10—Faith

You have the faith to move mountains. You can literally do anything to which you set your mind. Then why does faith fail? The problem is not a lack of faith. The problem is doubt. But one day you will know, beyond a shadow of a doubt, that you can accomplish anything in Christ.

> The apostles said to the Lord, "Increase our faith!"
>
> Luke 17:5 (NIV)

August 11—Lift Each Other Up

Our words can hurt or heal. Therefore, be excellent to each other through kindness. It is God's wish.

> Therefore encourage one another and build each other up, just as in fact you are doing.
>
> 1 Thessalonians 5:11 (NIV)

August 12—Life Is Temporal

Seize every opportunity to live; tomorrow is not promised.

> Show me, O Lord, my life's end and the number of my days; let me know how fleeting is my life.
>
> Psalm 39:4 (niv)

August 13—Job

Although God gave Job over to the power of the Enemy, the Lord still was keeping track of every hair on Job's head. The purpose of Job's trial was to see if he would keep the faith. He did. Even though he complained against God, he remained faithful by not taking his own life.

> But this is what you concealed in your heart, and I know that this was in your mind: If I sinned, you would be watching me and would not let my offense go unpunished.
>
> Job 10:13–14 (niv)

August 14—Pride

Prosperity can lead to pride, and pride precedes the fall. Remain humble in your prosperity. If you become too proud, you can lose it all.

> After Rehoboam's position as king was established and he had become strong, he and all Israel with him abandoned the law of the Lord.
>
> 2 Chronicles 12:1 (niv)

August 15—What It Takes

Christian salvation is based on Christ taking the blame for the sins of every man and dying in our place. Three days later, through the power of the Holy Spirit, Christ overpowered death and gave those who say that Christ is Lord the right to live in eternal paradise.

> That if you confess with your mouth, "Jesus is Lord," and believe in your heart that God raised him from the dead, you will be saved.
>
> Romans 10:9 (NIV)

August 16—Responsibility

Knowledge, insight and wisdom are three of the most powerful responsibilities a person can have. If you are given the talent of great wisdom, God will expect you to produce great things.

> But the one who does not know and does things deserving punishment will be beaten with few blows. From everyone who has been given much, much will be demanded; and from the one who has been entrusted with much, much more will be asked.
>
> Luke 12:48 (NIV)

August 17—The Law of Use

The law of use states that the more you use a talent, the stronger it becomes. But it is an unfaithful person who does nothing with his abilities. One day, he will want to do something great with his life and find out that his window of opportunity is shut.

> He replied, "I tell you that to everyone who has, more will be given, but as for the one who has nothing, even what he has will be taken away."
>
> Luke 19:26 (NIV)

August 18—Eternal Conflict

This life will feature internal and external struggles, but overall, the war is over—Christ is victorious!

> The thief comes only to steal and kill and destroy; I have come that they may have life, and have it to the full.
>
> John 10:10 (NIV)

August 19—Glory

Christ's victory at Calvary is so momentous that it not only affects our eternal destiny, but our earthly lives as well. Because of what Christ has done, we can live our lives in peaceful prosperity, knowing that we will always be taken care of.

> Therefore, since we have been justified through faith, we have peace with God through our Lord Jesus Christ, through whom we have gained access by faith into this grace in which we now stand. And we rejoice in the hope of the glory of God.
>
> Romans 5:1–2 (NIV)

August 20—Ease

The former high priests of the Old Testament had to prepare themselves for hours just before they could enter the area that God had designated for worship. Today, because of Christ's sacrifice, we can come into the holy presence of the all-powerful God at a moment's notice.

> The Lord said to Moses: "Tell your brother Aaron not to come whenever he chooses into the Most Holy Place behind the curtain in front of the atonement cover on the ark, or else he will die, because I appear in the cloud over the atonement cover."
>
> Leviticus 16:2 (NIV)

August 21—Enjoy

For many people, the words *work* and *enjoyment* are seldom found together. But using your talents is what gives fulfillment. God loved creating the universe and enjoys maintaining it. Be glad to be a part of the plan.

> God made the wild animals according to their kinds, the livestock according to their kinds, and all the creatures that move along the ground according to their kinds. And God saw that it was good.
>
> Genesis 1:25 (NIV)

August 22—Loss

Solomon lost his peace and spirituality after committing several sins of the flesh which compromised his integrity. He neglected his own wisdom and was ruined by sin.

> "Meaningless! Meaningless!" says the Teacher. "Utterly meaningless! Everything is meaningless."
>
> Ecclesiastes 1:2 (NIV)

August 23—Ready?

God is a loving, all-knowing, deeply devoted Father who wants the best for his children. He knows if we've been faithful. Are you ready for him to ask you about the decisions you've made in your life yet? What areas in your life still need improvement? Don't wait! Seek God and ask for his help in overcoming your shortcomings.

> So then, each of us will give an account of himself to God.
>
> Romans 14:12 (NIV)

August 24—Persecution

The reason we are forced to suffer in the world is because of the good we have done in the name of the Lord, whether we know it or not. Every time you do something nice for someone else, it's an attack on the kingdom of darkness. The devil will fight back, so be prepared in your heart for the blows inherent in the life of a Christian soldier.

> Blessed are you when people insult you, persecute you and falsely say all kinds of evil against you because of me.
>
> Matthew 5:11 (NIV)

August 25—Meekness

A sinner who is aware of his sins is better off than a sinner who is self-righteous. The self-righteous sinner often condemns others while ignoring his own transgressions. But a sinner who acknowledges his sins dwells in a glass house and knows better than to throw stones.

> But go and learn what this means: "I desire mercy, not sacrifice." For I have not come to call the righteous, but sinners.
>
> Matthew 9:13 (NIV)

August 26—Faith

You don't have to know many answers to be of use to God. All he requires from us is that we believe him when he shows us the truth.

> Abram believed the LORD, and he credited it to him as righteousness.
>
> Genesis 15:6 (NIV)

August 27—Letting Go

Believing God is sometimes a personal challenge. Not everything the Lord has to tell us is pleasant.

Sometimes the truth hurts. But if God is saying something, it means that we need to know it; there is no use in ignoring God. If he tells you to stop doing something you've gotten into the habit of doing and like doing, the sooner you let it go the better.

> Produce fruit in keeping with repentance. And do not begin to say to yourselves, "We have Abraham as our father." For I tell you that out of these stones God can raise up children for Abraham.
>
> Luke 3:8 (NIV)

August 28—On Guard

A person's heart is most happy when free from sin.

> Above all else, guard your heart, for it is the wellspring of life.
>
> Proverbs 4:23 (NIV)

August 29—Humility

It's better to let others praise you than to offer yourself the sacrifice of praise.

> For everyone who exalts himself will be humbled, and he who humbles himself will be exalted.
>
> Luke 14:11 (NIV)

August 30—Priorities

It is easy to get tied up in the pleasure of this world when you are young, but to resist pleasure's pull is noble. Choosing to put God's agenda over your own will give you an enjoyable life full of surprises.

> Remember your Creator in the days of your youth, before the days of trouble come and the years approach when you will say, "I find no pleasure in them."
>
> Ecclesiastes 12:1 (NIV)

August 31—The Love of a Child

Nothing is more rewarding than raising a child who does what is right. God loves it when he looks at his children and can say, "That's my child!" with pride.

> Honor your father and your mother, so that you may live long in the land the LORD your God is giving you.
>
> Exodus 20:12 (NIV)

September

September 1—The Tongue

The human tongue can do a great deal of good or harm. Therefore, speak wisely and allow your heart to stand guard over the things that come out of your mouth. You rarely need to apologize for something you have not said.

> The tongue also is a fire, a world of evil among the parts of the body. It corrupts the whole person, sets the whole course of his life on fire, and is itself set on fire by hell.
>
> James 3:6 (NIV)

September 2—Jesus's Prayer

Jesus prayed for the unity of the church. How can a body survive if one part abuses another? We must be gracious and excellent to each other; for that is the will of God.

> My prayer is not for them alone. I pray also for those who will believe in me through their message, that all of them may be one, Father, just as you are in me and I am in you. May they also be in us so that the world may believe that you have sent me.
>
> John 17:20–21 (NIV)

September 3—The Point of Scripture

If you want to know the difference between a person's point of view and God's truth, you must be aware of the prophesies of Old Testament Scripture and be familiar with the gospel and letters of the New Testament. It is important to study God's Word daily.

> All Scripture is God-breathed and is useful for teaching, rebuking, correcting and training in righteousness, so that the man of God may be thoroughly equipped for every good work.
>
> 2 Timothy 3:16–17 (NIV)

September 4—God's Love

Love is the most important thing in life. If you know people who are bitter-hearted and they act hateful toward you, they are only doing what comes naturally to them. Pay them no mind.

> I do not accept praise from men, but I know you. I know that you do not have the love of God in your hearts.
>
> John 5:41–42 (NIV)

September 5—Being Agreeable

People who are constantly arguing are outside the will of God. People who are true believers do not argue much; they help.

> Do everything without complaining or arguing, so that you may become blameless and pure, children of God without fault in a crooked and depraved generation, in which you shine like stars in the universe
>
> Philippians 2:14–15 (NIV)

September 6—God's Reach

Through his Holy Spirit, God can reach anyone he desires. Even some Pharisees followed Jesus, albeit in secret.

> Now there was a man of the Pharisees named Nicodemus, a member of the Jewish ruling council. He came to Jesus at night and said, "Rabbi, we know you are a teacher who has come from God. For no one could perform the miraculous signs you are doing if God were not with him."
>
> John 3:1–2 (NIV)

September 7—Wisdom

No matter what people say against you, God will give you the wisdom to show them in the wrong.

> But make up your mind not to worry beforehand

how you will defend yourselves. For I will give you words and wisdom that none of your adversaries will be able to resist or contradict.

Luke 21:14–15 (NIV)

September 8—The Benefits of Positivity

When we do our best with what we have to serve the Lord, God will always bless us. Even if it takes some time, wait with joyful expectancy. Joseph knew that God had promised him greatness, even when he was unjustly imprisoned. He stayed positive, received favor from the chief jailor, and was finally released into the fulfillment of God's promise after several years. The key to success over trials and tribulations in this life is patience and a positive attitude.

> When his master heard the story his wife told him, saying, "This is how your slave treated me," he burned with anger. Joseph's master took him and put him in prison, the place where the king's prisoners were confined. But while Joseph was there in the prison, the Lord was with him; he showed him kindness and granted him favor in the eyes of the prison warden.
>
> Genesis 39: 19–21 (NIV)

September 9—Don't Despair

Even in our darkest hour, we may still feel hopeful in knowing that the Lord will keep us safe. Just because things look bad doesn't mean that they'll stay that way.

> Moses answered the people, "Do not be afraid. Stand firm and you will see the deliverance the LORD will bring you today. The Egyptians you see today you will never see again."
>
> Exodus 14:13 (NIV)

September 10—An "A" for Attitude

Being all you can be differs from person to person. For some, it may be being the best teacher, preacher, painter, or poet, but what we all have as a general command for our lives is that we all must imitate Christ's behavior and overall attitude. God values those among us who possess a true servant's heart.

> Your attitude should be the same as that of Christ Jesus: Who, being in very nature God, did not consider equality with God some thing to be grasped, but made himself nothing, taking the very nature of a servant, being made in human likeness.
>
> Philippians 2:5–7 (NIV)

September 11—The Day

Our faith was shaken this day in 2001 but not destroyed. Our resolve was tested and came forth true. Christ watches over us always and cares for his people in eternity. God does not explain everything; therefore we can only believe that he will take this horrible memory and work it out for the good of the world through Christ Jesus, who cares for all things in the universe—including America.

> For by him all things were created: things in heaven and on earth, visible and invisible, whether thrones or powers or rulers or authorities; all things were created by him and for him. He is before all things, and in him all things hold together.
>
> Colossians 1:16–17 (NIV)

September 12—Prosperity

We are tested over how well we handle the abundances God gives, as well as how well we handle matters when supplies seem insufficient. God wants us to be like him: faithful at all times.

> Be careful that you do not forget the LORD your God, failing to observe his commands, his laws and his decrees that I am giving you this day.
>
> Deuteronomy 8:11 (NIV)

September 13—Giants

We all face obstacles in life that prevent us from getting what we want. But if you have a dream, a hope, or an aspiration that is divinely inspired, you are well able to overcome all obstacles on your way to that goal.

> Then I said to you, "Do not be terrified; do not be afraid of them. The LORD your God, who is going before you, will fight for you, as he did for you in Egypt, before your very eyes, and in the desert. There you saw how the LORD your God carried

you, as a father carries his son, all the way you went until you reached this place."

Deuteronomy 1:29–31 (NIV)

September 14—Love

Being aware that God loves you will give you the strength to love people. If you love others, you are fulfilling the commands God gave Moses. This command is especially difficult when it comes to loving the unlovely. In tough circumstances, such as those, pray for sufficient grace to get you through.

> See that what you have heard from the beginning remains in you. If it does, you also will remain in the Son and in the Father.
>
> 1 John 2:24 (NIV)

September 15—Like Father Like Sons

We need to be careful to set apart time every day to be alone with God. He gives us opportunities to be like him: holy. Holiness gives far more satisfaction than sinfulness; plus, holiness, which stems from a lifetime of belief, grants eternal security.

> Therefore, prepare your minds for action; be self-controlled; set your hope fully on the grace to be given you when Jesus Christ is revealed. As obedient children, do not conform to the evil desires you had when you lived in ignorance. But just as he who called you is holy, so be holy in all you do.
>
> 1 Peter 1:13–15 (NIV)

September 16—True Beauty

God is in all things. That's part of his description (omnipresent, all places at all times). That includes our fragile bodies. God sees what you see, hears what you hear, and tastes the food you taste. Therefore, we must do our best to make our bodies temples that are fitting for the Most High God: peaceful and free from fear.

> Your beauty should not come from outward adornment, such as braided hair and the wearing of gold jewelry and fine clothes. Instead, it should be that of your inner self, the unfading beauty of a gentle and quiet spirit, which is of great worth in God's sight.
>
> 1 Peter 3:3–4 (NIV)

September 17—The Most Important Thing

Our top priority should be to love one another. When you put love first, you will be satisfied; those who choose to obey God become truly content.

> Let no debt remain outstanding, except the continuing debt to love one another, for he who loves his fellowman has fulfilled the law.
>
> Romans 13:8 (NIV)

September 18—Fair-Weather Believers

Why do you worship God? Is it out of respect? Think. Have your motives ever been tested? Only then, only through hard times, will you know the fortitude of your faith.

> But stretch out your hand and strike everything he has, and he will surely curse you to your face.
>
> Job 1:11 (NIV)

September 19—Hard Times

The world in which we live can sometimes be like a roller coaster without safety belts. This place is wild. Today, cling to God; love and obey him. Pray to God when you are hurting. Give thanks for having the breath for thanksgiving. And remember: this too shall pass.

> Consider it pure joy, my brothers, whenever you face trials of many kinds, because you know that the testing of your faith develops perseverance.
>
> James 1:2–3 (NIV)

September 20—What's in It for Me?

You give money, time, and talent to serve the greater good. But what are you getting in return? Think. Are you at peace in a war-plagued world? Are you able to be nice when others are unkind? You will be rewarded in this life and the life to come, guaranteed.

> Peter answered him, "We have left everything to follow you! What then will there be for us?" Jesus said to them, "I tell you the truth, at the renewal of all things, when the Son of Man sits on his glo-

rious throne, you who have followed me will also sit on twelve thrones, judging the twelve tribes of Israel. And everyone who has left houses or brothers or sisters or father or mother or children or fields for my sake will receive a hundred times as much and will inherit eternal life. But many who are first will be last, and many who are last will be first."

Matthew 19:27–30 (NIV)

September 21—Blessings

The most valuable gift God gives his children is the assurance he has that tells us that everything is going to be all right.

> The Lord bless you and keep you; the Lord make his face shine upon you and be gracious to you; the Lord turn his face toward you and give you peace.
>
> Numbers 6:24–26 (NIV)

September 22—Covenant

God loves you and will not only bless you with wealth and give you peace of mind but will also give prosperity to those who are good to you.

> I will bless those who bless you, and whoever curses you I will curse; and all peoples on earth will be blessed through you.
>
> Genesis 12:3 (NIV)

September 23—Smile on Others

Goodness overcomes evil every time. An evil repaid leads to your blessing stopped or delayed.

> But I tell you who hear me: Love your enemies, do good to those who hate you, bless those who curse you, pray for those who mistreat you.
>
> Luke 6:27–28 (NIV)

September 24—Temple

God is in everything; he created everything, especially his people. God sees everything you see, hears everything you hear, and feels everything you feel. With that in mind, it is smart to surround yourself with goodness so that your conscience, God, will be at ease inside you. Making God's Spirit comfortable as he dwells in your soul is a good idea.

> Do you not know that your body is a temple of the Holy Spirit, who is in you, whom you have received from God? You are not your own; you were bought at a price. Therefore honor God with your body.
>
> 1 Corinthians 6:19–20 (NIV)

September 25—Meaning

When people pursue success instead of a relationship with God, no matter how much they earn, it will be meaningless. Opportunists won't enjoy their billions as much as a spiritual person will enjoy one hundred.

> Yet when I surveyed all that my hands had done and what I had toiled to achieve, everything was meaningless, a chasing after the wind; nothing was gained under the sun.
>
> Ecclesiastes 2:11 (NIV)

September 26—Rest

You may be in a routine that requires more from you than you have to give. But you will grow stronger. If you are facing too much resistance in life, retreat to the Lord, and he will give you rest.

> Come to me, all you who are weary and burdened, and I will give you rest.
>
> Matthew 11:28 (NIV)

September 27—God Cares

There is so much gladness in heaven when someone on earth turns away from sin and turns toward Jesus.

> In the same way, I tell you, there is rejoicing in the presence of the angels of God over one sinner who repents.
>
> Luke 15:10 (NIV)

September 28—Get to Know the Lord

Think about your spouse. Did you always love her unconditionally? You probably began little by little and slowly developed a relationship that would last forever.

The same is true in Christianity. The more time you spend with Jesus, the deeper your love is for life itself.

> But grow in the grace and knowledge of our Lord and Savior Jesus Christ. To him be glory both now and forever! Amen.
>
> 2 Peter 3:18 (NIV)

September 29—The Temple of the Lord

King Solomon, son of King David, was commanded by God to design and build Israel's holy temple. You too have certain preordained projects to do in your lifetime that you can do better than anybody else. What are your talents? And imagine, what will be your legacy?

> Now, my son, the LORD be with you, and may you have success and build the house of the LORD your God, as he said you would.
>
> 1 Chronicles 22:11 (NIV)

September 30—Jesus Wants To

Why does a loving God permit good people to suffer? There are many reasons. Firstly, it gives us a chance to grow closer to the Holy One. The most important thing between God and humans is relationship. Once a relationship is established, there is no telling what blessings God will pour on you.

Jesus reached out his hand and touched the man. "I am willing," he said. "Be clean!" Immediately he was cured of his leprosy.

>Matthew 8:3 (NIV)

October

October 1—Sin and Redemption

Every person on earth has been born into a fallen world, ridden with the blackness of sin. The evil powers of this world would like you to make things worse, but that would be a mistake, because God punishes sin with death. Jesus died so that you would have the Spirit to avoid temptation, and spend eternity in peace.

> For the wages of sin is death, but the gift of God is eternal life in Christ Jesus our Lord.
>
> Romans 6:23 (NIV)

October 2—God Knows You

God knows everything you have ever done; God knows everything you will ever do. And through it all, he loves you with open arms.

> Before I formed you in the womb I knew you, before you were born I set you apart; I appointed you as a prophet to the nations.
>
> Jeremiah 1:5 (NIV)

October 3—Godly Recompense

God will reward you for all the good things you have done in this life. All of the things you have done for people who were unable to help themselves will be rewarded, and your eternal reward will satisfy you completely.

> But when you give a banquet, invite the poor, the crippled, the lame, the blind, and you will be blessed. Although they cannot repay you, you will be repaid at the resurrection of the righteous.
>
> Luke 14:13–14 (NIV)

October 4—God's Promise

God never promised us an easy life, but he did promise that he would always be with us to help us through our difficulties, temptations, and trials. No matter how hard life gets, there is a loving God who can't fail his people.

> No one will be able to stand up against you all the days of your life. As I was with Moses, so I will be with you; I will never leave you nor forsake you.
>
> Joshua 1:5 (NIV)

October 5—True Repentance

When you ask for forgiveness, God will forgive you. And the best way to say thank you is to learn a lesson from the pain your mistakes have caused you.

> Produce fruit in keeping with repentance.
>
> Matthew 3:8 (NIV)

October 6—Perfection

Excellence in life comes through practice and discipline. We will always need God in this world because he is the Author and Finisher of our faith and the only means to our becoming, eventually, flawless.

> Be perfect, therefore, as your heavenly Father is perfect.
>
> Matthew 5:48 (NIV)

October 7—Jesus

Jesus suffered temptation in the desert. In forty days, he experienced every temptation known to man. In three hours, he experienced the punishment of every sin ever committed—past, present, and future. He suffered worse than Job, and never sinned in word, thought, or deed. He was totally blameless, absolutely perfect.

> At once the Spirit sent him out into the desert, and he was in the desert forty days, being tempted

by Satan. He was with the wild animals, and angels attended him.

> Mark 1:12–13 (NIV)

October 8—Godliness

Being good leads to health and safety. Whereas evil actions remove a person's reason for hope and steal peace of mind.

> Righteousness guards the man of integrity, but wickedness overthrows the sinner.
>
> Proverbs 13:6 (NIV)

October 9—Meekness

Even though some people seem more important than others according to the world's standard, we are all of equal value in God's sight because we were all bought by Christ's blood.

> For we were all baptized by one Spirit into one body—whether Jews or Greeks, slave or free—and we were all given the one Spirit to drink.
>
> 1 Corinthians 12:13 (NIV)

October 10—God's Plan

God's good, positive, and liberating design for your life cannot be undone by adverse circumstances or failure. What we must do is remember that no matter how bad things get, the Lord is strong, and he is your defender.

I have set the Lord always before me. Because he is at my right hand, I will not be shaken.

Psalm 16:8 (NIV)

October 11—Paying it Forward

God allows good people to suffer because they will learn from their suffering and will have firsthand experience to pass on to others in need; the suffering of the righteous leads to good.

> Praise be to the God and Father of our Lord Jesus Christ, the Father of compassion and the God of all comfort, who comforts us in all our troubles, so that we can comfort those in any trouble with the comfort we ourselves have received from God.
>
> 2 Corinthians 1:3–4 (NIV)

October 12—The Choice Is Yours

Everyone will be remembered for the choices they have made and the things they have taken a stand for. Whom you serve determines your eternal reward.

> But if serving the Lord seems undesirable to you, then choose for yourselves this day whom you will serve, whether the gods your forefathers served beyond the River, or the gods of the Amorites, in whose land you are living. But as for me and my household, we will serve the Lord.
>
> Joshua 24:15 (NIV)

October 13—Trust

God can do for man what man can't do for himself. God can provide power to do any job, no matter how impossible. God can give man a quiet, stress-free heart in the most horrifying of circumstances. And God can change the heart of even the most insufferable sinner. Today God will help you. Just ask.

> Commit your way to the Lord; trust in him and he will do this:
> He will make your righteousness shine like the dawn, the justice of your cause like the noonday sun.
>
> Psalm 37:5 (NIV)

October 14—Snide Remarks

Jesus chose to ignore the unfriendly remarks from people rather than justify himself. The Lord our God is our vindicator, and he will justify us if we trust him by not taking matters into our own hands.

> Ignoring what they said, Jesus told the synagogue ruler, "Don't be afraid; just believe."
>
> Mark 5:36 (NIV)

October 15—Mercy

Jonathan Edwards once said that the man who has not prayed for God's mercy has no more strength to keep himself out of hell than a spider's web could stop a boulder.

Because of the LORD's great love we are not consumed, for his compassions never fail.

> Lamentations 3:22 (NIV)

October 16—Choose a Side

Hot coffee is good, and so is iced coffee; both sell for over a dollar. But imagine a coffee vendor selling tepid coffee. People would take one sip and say, This is unacceptable! Our Father is no different. God does not do things halfway, lukewarm, and he expects us to go all the way with our efforts as well.

> I know your deeds, that you are neither cold nor hot. I wish you were either one or the other!
>
> Revelation 3:15 (NIV)

October 17—Courage under Fire

There is no better favor we can bestow upon ourselves than to pray for those who hurt us. The attitude that says, I've been hurt, so I will hurt back, is natural but not helpful. We poison ourselves when offense is taken. And someday, God will make it right.

> It may be that the LORD will see my distress and repay me with good for the cursing I am receiving today.
>
> 2 Samuel 16:12 (NIV)

October 18—Prayer Power

Confession of sin leads to joy because God makes us righteous when we ask him for forgiveness. Righteousness leads to peace, and peace ushers in joy; with joy, we feel great strength and power through the Holy Spirit. The prayer coming from a righteous heart receives a prompt response from God.

> Therefore confess your sins to each other and pray for each other so that you may be healed. The prayer of a righteous man is powerful and effective.
>
> James 5:16 (NIV)

October 19—How We Survive

In life, there will be heated battles that you will face. Maybe even today you will have your faith tested. But bear in mind that even the hardest test is only that: a test. Humility, patience, and trust in God are all you need to pass through safely. And remember, even when it feels as if God is far away, he is still caring for you.

> Those who trust in the LORD are like Mount Zion, which cannot be shaken but endures forever.
>
> Psalm 125:1 (NIV)

October 20—Prayer

The secret of living in a world plagued by sin is to draw on God's love at all times. Jesus prayed for hours before and after every day so that he would be powerful enough to handle the people's needs. If God in the flesh had to pray, then we must pray as well. Prayer fills people with God's power and love. When full of the Holy Spirit, people need less from the world and are capable of giving more to it.

> Let us then approach the throne of grace with confidence, so that we may receive mercy and find grace to help us in our time of need.
>
> Hebrews 4:16 (NIV)

October 21—Words

You have a heavy responsibility to say what is good and to deny yourself the temptation of speaking sinfully. It is devastatingly frightening to comprehend the power we are accountable for every time we open our mouths to speak. How easy it is to kill with words, and how simple it is to bring joy! Choose your words wisely.

> We all stumble in many ways. If anyone is never at fault in what he says, he is a perfect man, able to keep his whole body in check.
>
> James 3:2 (NIV)

October 22—Ultimate Victory

If you ever feel alone, separated, and full of sorrow, just remember the fact that life puts us through unfavorable circumstances for our overall good, so that we may learn. And in the end, we win.

> I have told you these things, so that in me you may have peace. In this world you will have trouble. But take heart! I have overcome the world."
>
> John 16:33 (NIV)

October 23—You are Divine Artwork

You have more to offer than you can even imagine. You are more powerful than you can conceive. Don't waste energy feeling inferior to anyone, because God has gifted everyone with unique talents. Discover your abilities and make your mark.

> For we are God's workmanship, created in Christ Jesus to do good works, which God prepared in advance for us to do.
>
> Ephesians 2:10 (NIV)

October 24—Be Nice

There is a reason why Jesus told us to love our neighbors as we love ourselves. Believe in the principle of reaping and sowing. If you treat one person badly, that will end with you being treated badly when you least expect it. Therefore, be nice.

> For in the same way you judge others, you will be judged, and with the measure you use, it will be measured to you.
>
> Matthew 7:2 (NIV)

October 25—Serve

In keeping with the principle of reaping and sowing, serve others so that you may receive help from people when you need it.

> Just as the Son of Man did not come to be served, but to serve, and to give his life as a ransom for many.
>
> Matthew 20:28 (NIV)

October 26—God Already Knows

If you've got a habit that nobody knows about, God knows. Pay now, or pay later, but eventually everybody doing things against God's will for their lives pays a high price. Therefore, take inventory of and remove sin.

> For there is nothing hidden that will not be disclosed, and nothing concealed that will not be known or brought out into the open.
>
> Luke 8:17 (NIV)

October 27—Protection

No matter how people try to hurt you, the Lord will rescue you from their clutches (generally after much pain and suffering). Take comfort in knowing that suffering produces endurance and makes us wiser. God will take your problem and turn it into your power.

> Let those who love the LORD hate evil, for he guards the lives of his faithful ones and delivers them from the hand of the wicked.
>
> Psalm 97:10 (NIV)

October 28—Two Sides

Don't hold it against yourself for having bad ideas flash across your mind. They're as much a part of you as anything else. No good person wants this to be true, but it's a comfort to know that God doesn't expect perfect performance, just an exemplary desire to overcome sin.

> For the sinful nature desires what is contrary to the Spirit, and the Spirit what is contrary to the sinful nature. They are in conflict with each other, so that you do not do what you want.
>
> Galatians 5:17 (NIV)

October 29—Ocular Adultery

Fantasizing about someone other than your wife is almost as bad as doing it.

> But I tell you that anyone who looks at a woman lustfully has already committed adultery with her in his heart.
>
> Matthew 5:28 (NIV)

October 30—Your Lifeline

Imagine your life on earth compared to the deep sea divers of old. When man first explored the depths of the ocean, he wore a massive suit with a mask that had air pumped into it from a boat. Now imagine if that air tube was severed. Our air tube is our relationship with God, and sin is the knife that cuts it off.

> But your iniquities have separated you from your God; your sins have hidden his face from you, so that he will not hear.
>
> Isaiah 59:2 (NIV)

October 31—Integrity

God doesn't consider the theft of two pennies any less of a sin than the theft of two million. Theft is theft, and sin is sin.

> Whoever can be trusted with very little can also be trusted with much, and whoever is dishonest with very little will also be dishonest with much.
>
> Luke 16:10 (NIV)

November

November 1—Wholehearted Repentance

When we are faced with a decision to continue in the wrong direction or to make a U-turn and get things right, obstacles are bound to come up that will try to stop you from returning to God's way of handling life. As a result, you will have to work twice as hard just to repent. But God promises guaranteed results for those who practice wholehearted repentance.

> And Samuel said to the whole house of Israel, "If you are returning to the LORD with all your hearts, then rid yourselves of the foreign gods and the Ashtoreths and commit yourselves to the LORD and serve him only, and he will deliver you out of the hand of the Philistines."
>
> 1 Samuel 7:3 (NIV)

November 2—Doing Things though Afraid

Jesus felt fear when it came time for him to face his fate. He sweated drops of blood while praying to God for another way. But he did his work God's way, regardless. Being brave doesn't mean an absolute absence of fear; it means that you would rather die than fail to try.

> As the time approached for him to be taken up to heaven, Jesus resolutely set out for Jerusalem.
>
> Luke 9:51 (NIV)

November 3—Right Choices

The knowledge between right and wrong is a gift given to someone after a long period of holiness, in which a person continuously made right choices while temptations appeared appetizing.

> But solid food is for the mature, who by constant use have trained themselves to distinguish good from evil.
>
> Hebrews 5:14 (NIV)

November 4—Work Hard

When we put everything we have into a task, keeping in mind that we are earthly servants working for heaven, it doesn't matter what we do. You could shovel coal or be an ambassador to foreign nations. The point is that all work is honorable, and we all must strive to do our best.

> Whatever you do, work at it with all your heart, as working for the Lord, not for men, since you know that you will receive an inheritance from the Lord as a reward. It is the Lord Christ you are serving.
>
> Colossians 3:23–24 (NIV)

November 5—Your Task

While going about your day, you are bound to come across at least one person in need of encouragement. They may express a direct or indirect need, but the least we can do for God is use our strength to comfort others.

> Therefore encourage one another and build each other up, just as in fact you are doing.
>
> 1 Thessalonians 5:11 (NIV)

November 6—Have Hope

You will face uncomfortable circumstances; that's a promise. The Lord will allow the world to tempt you so that he will know your intentions; that's a guarantee. God does not tempt us because he cannot be tempted, and whenever temptation becomes a factor, God will show us a way out. When you prove trustworthy to the Lord, he will reward you both on earth and in heaven; that too is a promise—don't give up.

> In this you greatly rejoice, though now for a little while you may have had to suffer grief in all kinds of trials.
>
> 1 Peter 1:6 (NIV)

November 7—True Ministry

It may be difficult to remain levelheaded when it seems as though the whole world's coming down on you, but Jesus told us that no slave is greater than his master. If he suffered, then we will too. But the comfort is in knowing that God has a reason for permitting suffering; suffering is training. And in the end, when you don't quit, you will be able to complete the work that God has given you to do.

> But you, keep your head in all situations, endure hardship, do the work of an evangelist, discharge all the duties of your ministry.
>
> 2 Timothy 4:5 (NIV)

November 8—Endure

No matter how much suffering this world can deliver, nothing compares with the prize of eternal life in God's presence. Keep that in mind when you are being afflicted for your beliefs.

> All men will hate you because of me, but he who stands firm to the end will be saved.
>
> Matthew 10:22 (NIV)

November 9—Love Your Neighbor

It's difficult to suffer unjustly and still love your enemies, but that ability is a strength available to all believers through the power of the Holy Spirit. It's what Jesus did, and he asks the same from his followers.

> You have heard that it was said, "Love your neighbor and hate your enemy." But I tell you: Love your enemies and pray for those who persecute you, that you may be sons of your Father in heaven. He causes his sun to rise on the evil and the good, and sends rain on the righteous and the unrighteous.
>
> Matthew 5:43–44 (NIV)

November 10 —Desire

You can show God your love and devotion by continuing to do the work he gave you with a good attitude. Many people keep doing their God-given work but, without heartfelt gladness at the opportunity to serve him. Without a desire to serve God, God would rather you didn't do anything.

> Yet I hold this against you: You have forsaken your first love.
>
> Revelation 2:4 (NIV)

November 11—Temptation

Any seductive sensation that puts you out of the will of God is temptation. And temptation is the fecal matter of sin wrapped in shiny paper.

> No temptation has seized you except what is common to man. And God is faithful; he will not let you be tempted beyond what you can bear. But when you are tempted, he will also provide a way out so that you can stand up under it.
>
> 1 Corinthians 10:13 (NIV)

November 12—God's Promise

Have you ever had a dream come true? A long-anticipated wish actualized? Before those dreams came true, were there times of doubt when it seemed as if God was never going to deliver you into the promised land? But then he did! And look how much better off you are now than you were back then. God is always looking to bless the faithful. Who's to say that your next series of dreams won't come true? Too many people quit dreaming—don't be one of them.

> For the revelation awaits an appointed time; it speaks of the end and will not prove false. Though it linger, wait for it; it will certainly come and will not delay.
>
> Habakkuk 2:3 (NIV)

November 13—Alone

Being alone in God's presence is necessary. Without time for prayer and meditation, life would be too hectic for living. If Jesus had to pray, then everyone has a need to pray as well.

> After he had dismissed them, he went up on a mountainside by himself to pray. When evening came, he was there alone,
>
> Matthew 14:23 (NIV)

November 14—Heaven's Citizens

The prophet Isaiah prophesized about the future

inhabitants of heaven. Imagine a place where nobody lies, cheats or steals. Sometimes the greatest gifts are things that the Lord takes away.

> He who walks righteously and speaks what is right, who rejects gain from extortion and keeps his hand from accepting bribes, who stops his ears against plots of murder and shuts his eyes against contemplating evil.
>
> Isaiah 33:15 (NIV)

November 15— Impossible Is Nothing to God

Just because circumstances seem daunting and formidable does not mean they are hopeless. In fact, when things are at their worst is usually when a miracle occurs. Don't despair; you'll get through this.

> As Pharaoh approached, the Israelites looked up, and there were the Egyptians, marching after them. They were terrified and cried out to the LORD. They said to Moses, "Was it because there were no graves in Egypt that you brought us to the desert to die? What have you done to us by bringing us out of Egypt?
>
> Exodus 14:10–11 (NIV)

November 16—Faith versus Unbelief

Jesus said that if one were to have faith the size of a mustard seed, then he could cast a mountain into the sea. Faith works. What keeps people from living in victory is the doubts placed in their minds by a variety of voices in society meant to disquiet a person's spirituality.

> Immediately the boy's father exclaimed, "I do believe; help me overcome my unbelief!"
>
> Mark 9:24 (NIV)

November 17—Stand Firm

The onramp to heaven is long and features many tempting places to pull over and stop. But the Lord wants us to keep moving toward the prize he has set in front of us. He takes no pleasure in quitters.

> But my righteous one will live by faith. And if he shrinks back, I will not be pleased with him.
>
> Hebrews 10:38 (NIV)

November 18—Seeing the Unseen

Many times in life, I have had opportunities that were very possible and likely to blossom into actualities, but I would agonize over the possibility of being denied my wish. Although it all took a long time to happen, God has given me everything I have ever truly wanted and continues to provide.

> Now faith is being sure of what we hope for and certain of what we do not see.
>
> Hebrews 11:1 (NIV)

November 19—Change of Heart

When you are a righteous believer, it really doesn't matter what anybody else has to say about you. You'll do more in your life than any of those bitter people, who can only criticize what they don't understand. If you have a clean conscience, feel free to follow it.

> No, a man is a Jew if he is one inwardly; and circumcision is circumcision of the heart, by the Spirit, not by the written code. Such a man's praise is not from men, but from God.
>
> Romans 2:29 (NIV)

November 20—God's Provisions

God has some big ideas for his children. His plans are so great that not even the smartest spiritual leader can understand God's entire plan for one single day, for one single person, no less the entire world. Take comfort in knowing that God is good, loving, and really smart. He will love you through even the most challenging parts of his plan for your development.

> For this reason I kneel before the Father, from whom his whole family in heaven and on earth derives its name.
>
> Ephesians 3:14–15 (NIV)

November 21—Judge Not

A person with wisdom knows that he is subject to any sin for the entire time he is on this planet. And while murder may be something not in your nature, you still don't have the right to judge; maybe you are capable of something worse if the circumstances were bad enough.

> Do not judge, or you too will be judged. For in the same way you judge others, you will be judged, and with the measure you use, it will be measured to you.
>
> Matthew 7:1–2 (NIV)

November 22—God's Will

God is kind. He will only ask us to do what will help us. By doing what God says in the Bible, we are assured victory. God does not ask us to work for him because he needs the help; rather, God asks us to do things that will make us enjoy our lives more.

> And now, O Israel, what does the LORD your God ask of you but to fear the LORD your God, to walk in all his ways, to love him, to serve the LORD your God with all your heart and with all your soul, and to observe the LORD's commands and decrees that I am giving you today for your own good?
>
> Deuteronomy 10: 12–13 (NIV)

November 23—Direction

Trusting God in trying circumstances is right. And when you see your troubles passing away, it becomes obvious that God was near the whole time, steering you in the right direction.

> Who, then, is the man that fears the LORD?
> He will instruct him in the way chosen for him.
>
> Psalm 25:12 (NIV)

November 24—Majestic Sovereign Power

Even when things seem bad, God is working and fighting for you behind the scenes. It is our responsibility not to take matters into our own hands in a way that would bring shame upon ourselves and the name of the Lord.

> Moses said to the people, "Do not be afraid. God has come to test you, so that the fear of God will be with you to keep you from sinning."
>
> Exodus 20:20 (NIV)

November 25—God's Protection

It's the world's responsibility, it seems, to make good people worry and suffer. The temptation to react irrationally to a potentially hazardous circumstance must be overridden by prayer. Don't make matters worse by acting outside God's will. He will lead you through the illusion of disaster. The worst threat we face in life is our own overreactions to a perceived threat. Just relax., God loves you and will see you through with blessings to spare.

> After this, the word of the LORD came to Abram in a vision: "Do not be afraid, Abram. I am your shield, your very great reward."
>
> Genesis 15:1 (NIV)

November 26—Be Brave

Jesus told us that the world would make us suffer but to take heart because he has overcome the world. The worst thing we will face is temporary, and the reward for enduring is eternal. Therefore, we must pray so that we do not get overwhelmed with anxiety, doubts, and fear.

> For God did not give us a spirit of timidity, but a spirit of power, of love and of self-discipline.
>
> 2 Timothy 1:7 (NIV)

November 27—Fear No Man

People who abuse their power can be frightening and unnerving to deal with. But if you know God and know who you are in God's eyes, it makes no difference how much sway an individual may have in a given position. He will not be able to do any lasting damage to anyone who believes the truth of the Lord.

> Fear of man will prove to be a snare, but whoever trusts in the LORD is kept safe.
>
> Proverbs 29:25 (NIV)

November 28—Heaven on Earth

Forget your temporal worries and woes. Heaven awaits you!

> Set your minds on things above, not on earthly things.
>
> Colossians 3:2 (NIV)

November 29—Internal Conflict

Inside every believer is a raging war between good and evil. The good news is, however, that the more good a person does, the easier it becomes to continue doing good and that person becomes less and less likely to hear and be tempted by the old sinful nature.

> For the sinful nature desires what is contrary to the Spirit, and the Spirit what is contrary to the sinful nature. They are in conflict with each other, so that you do not do what you want.
>
> Galatians 5:17 (NIV)

November 30—The Kingdom of God

If you trust God with the eternal fate of your soul, why not trust him to provide for you while you're still living? God will stretch our faith, and like all growing, this will be uncomfortable; but it's worthwhile because there is freedom in that discomfort. It frees us up to seek the provision of the Lord while living a life, potentially, free from worry.

So do not worry, saying, "What shall we eat?" or "What shall we drink?" or "What shall we wear?" For the pagans run after all these things, and your heavenly Father knows that you need them. But seek first his kingdom and his righteousness, and all these things will be given to you as well.

        Matthew 6:31–33 (NIV)

December

December 1—Work Hard

The person who enthusiastically works to satisfy the Lord will experience satisfaction and a sense of prosperity in his soul. All who serve the Lord will continue living in this land for a real reason.

> Never be lacking in zeal, but keep your spiritual fervor, serving the Lord.
>
> Romans 12:11 (NIV)

December 2—When You Feel God Has Left You Alone

If Jesus felt as if God had abandoned him at a crucial moment in his earthly existence, then it is likely that Christians will feel disconnected from God sometimes. It happens to everybody, but it does not change God's unfailing grace to come through for us when we need it. If Jesus, quoting the prophet Isaiah, wondered why God had severed their connection, our momentary scares are understandable.

> And at the ninth hour Jesus cried out in a loud voice, "Eloi, Eloi, lama sabachthani?"—which means, "My God, my God, why have you forsaken me?"
>
> Mark 15:34 (NIV)

December 3—Real Freedom

True freedom is being able to do what your heart desires in accordance with the will of God. Christ must train us before he sets us loose on the world. The Bible tells us that no discipline is pleasant for the time being. But a disciplined person of character will have enough wisdom to live life free and clear of sin's traps.

> No discipline seems pleasant at the time, but painful. Later on, however, it produces a harvest of righteousness and peace for those who have been trained by it.
>
> Hebrews 12:11 (NIV)

December 4—God's Children

Jesus is the ultimate redeemer. Believe that he died so that you might live, believe in the things he spoke about in the gospels, and be considered a child of God, living in an eternal paradise.

> Yet to all who received him, to those who believed in his name, he gave the right to become children of God—
>
> John 1:12 (NIV)

December 5—False Rule and Regulations

The reason Jesus has set us free is so we can follow our hearts and obey the will of God. We are free to do good with our lives, and goodness brings about its own rewards, just as evil punishes the one who sins. The Law was written for sinners to know where they're wrong. But just as Jesus healed on the Sabbath, we too can disobey certain man-made rules if we feel it is God's will.

> It is for freedom that Christ has set us free. Stand firm, then, and do not let yourselves be burdened again by a yoke of slavery.
>
> Galatians 5:1 (NIV)

December 6—Friends of God

Jesus has a universe's amount of information to teach us, and now that we are free from the grip of sin, we will have a lot more time to get to know him. He teaches in many ways. He may have a song come on your radio with a lyric he knows you need to hear. He is always interacting with us. Do not complain then, just pray. He's right next to you.

> I no longer call you servants, because a servant does not know his master's business. Instead, I have called you friends, for everything that I learned from my Father I have made known to you.
>
> John 15:15 (NIV)

December 7—Marriage

Whether married or single, God has a good plan for you. Your marital status is not a status symbol. It just identifies the vows and promises you choose to live by. As long as you're serving God, you're going to be okay.

> I say this as a concession, not as a command. But I wish everyone were single, just as I am. But God gives to some the gift of marriage, and to others the gift of singleness.
>
> 1 Corinthians 7:6–7 (NLT)

December 8—Fruits of the Spirit

When you love, your life will be full of joy and peace. When at peace, you can afford to be patient and kind, and that is good. A person with the fruit of the spirit is living a good life, and he isn't breaking any laws. You really can be nice and still enjoy life. In fact it helps.

> But the fruit of the Spirit is love, joy, peace, patience, kindness, goodness, faithfulness, gentleness and self-control. Against such things there is no law.
>
> Galatians 5:22–23 (NIV)

December 9—Patience

The ability to relate to people on a personal level is crucial to being an effective Christian. It's the difficult people who need the most help, so be patient with them. If they're hard to get along with, chances are that they are hurting. Pray for some insight on how to help.

> And the Lord's servant must not quarrel; instead, he must be kind to everyone, able to teach, not resentful.
>
> 2 Timothy 2:24 (NIV)

December 10—Wisdom from Heaven

Being nice is the wisest action. But it takes time for people to get to the point where they are comfortable being nice when they would rather quarrel. The longer you act in kindness, the easier it will be to be like Jesus. And what used to make you angry will no longer have any effect.

> But the wisdom that comes from heaven is first of all pure; then peace-loving, considerate, submissive, full of mercy and good fruit, impartial and sincere.
>
> James 3:17 (NIV)

December 11—Triumph Over Adversity

Hard times make for sharp minds. Once you've been issued the rawest deals life can give and you've come out the other side victorious, there is nothing that will be able to intimidate you. And a fearless man of God is a threat to the devil, and he knows it.

> Therefore we do not lose heart. Though outwardly we are wasting away, yet inwardly we are being renewed day by day. For our light and momentary troubles are achieving for us an eternal glory that far outweighs them all.
>
> 2 Corinthians 4:16–17 (NIV)

December 12—Sorrowful Sin

Sin burdens everyone, especially God. Corruption and sin are meant to keep us from knowing right from wrong. A working knowledge between right and wrong determines our personal level of holiness. And holiness is a gift from God; it keeps us out of harm's way.

> The LORD was grieved that he had made man on the earth, and his heart was filled with pain. So the LORD said, "I will wipe mankind, whom I have created, from the face of the earth—men and animals, and creatures that move along the ground, and birds of the air—for I am grieved that I have made them." But Noah found favor in the eyes of the LORD.
>
> Genesis 6:6–8 (NIV)

December 13—Believe and Receive

The power of what you believe is so mighty that you can, through prayer to God, do anything to which you set your mind. God's not going to give you a million dollars in most instances, but he may give you the idea and the know-how that will get you a million dollars. God answers prayers in so many ways. That's why it pays to be open to God's creativity, and not be closed minded to his sovereign ability to make things happen.

> If you believe, you will receive whatever you ask for in prayer.
>
> Matthew 21:22 (NIV)

December 14—Obedience

In Jesus's Sermon on the Mount, he discusses true happiness. One of the avenues to true happiness is a sincere desire to do the will of God. Matthew 5:6 says, "Happy are those whose greatest desire is to do what God requires; God will satisfy them fully!" To do the work God has preordained for you to do is one of the greatest blessings in the universe.

> Therefore, my dear friends, as you have always obeyed—not only in my presence, but now much more in my absence—continue to work out your salvation with fear and trembling, for it is God who works in you to will and to act according to his good purpose.
>
> Philippians 2:12–13 (NIV)

December 15—
Why God Allows Bad Things

God allows bad things to happen to good people, but why? Maybe God wants someone to grow closer to him through adversity. Maybe God has tried to speak change into a person's life for a long time, and suffering is the only language left. Whatever the case may be, God is fair, and will never let more happen than a person can bear.

> In the land of Uz there lived a man whose name was Job. This man was blameless and upright; he feared God and shunned evil.
>
> Job 1:1 (NIV)

December 16—God's Intent

Joseph knew that all of his suffering and pain were necessary agents meant to prepare him for the job God wanted him to have. Being unjustly imprisoned and sold into slavery were bad things God allowed to happen to a good man, but God made good things come from those unfortunate instances. When you're trapped in the storm, remember that God can turn a test into an amazing testimony.

> You intended to harm me, but God intended it for good to accomplish what is now being done, the saving of many lives.
>
> Genesis 50:20 (NIV)

December 17—Heaven

We have the privilege of hope in exasperating circumstances. After Christ died and rose again, death no longer had the final word. If Christ had enough power to raise himself out of hell and back to life, how much more then will he be able to do the same for those who believe in him to save them.

> Brothers, we do not want you to be ignorant about those who fall asleep, or to grieve like the rest of men, who have no hope.
>
> 1 Thessalonians 4:13 (NIV)

December 18—Real Humility

If you are to look at our role model, Jesus, it is apparent that we are here to serve others. Just because you belong to God does not entitle you to have everything handed to you. God will give you the training you need to be of service to as many people as you choose to be accountable to. It is far more enjoyable to give than it is to receive.

> Your attitude should be the same as that of Christ Jesus: Who, being in very nature God, did not consider equality with God something to be grasped, but made himself nothing, taking the very nature of a servant, being made in human likeness.
>
> Philippians 2:5–7 (NIV)

December 19—Life Is Temporary

Whether your life is plagued by problems or brimming with blessings, take care of the things God has given you stewardship over. There will come a time when you no longer have to get up and go about your day in an earthly manner. At that time, you'll be standing in a long line that leads to the last account you will have to give, when God will either accept you into the eternity of paradise or condemn you. At that time, you will know what was truly valuable and what was a waste of time.

> Show me, O Lord, my life's end and the number of my days; let me know how fleeting is my life.
>
> Psalm 39:4 (NIV)

December 20—Faithful Deeds

There is a world of good to be done in this fallen world. But it takes years of study and practice to know how to consistently do the right thing. When you always make the right decision, you have arrived at holiness. This may sound impossible, but with God, all things are possible. Keep your mouth speaking positively, and your deeds will follow.

> With this in mind, we constantly pray for you, that our God may count you worthy of his calling, and that by his power he may fulfill every good purpose of yours and every act prompted by your faith.
>
> 2 Thessalonians 1:11 (NIV)

December 21—Don't Forget

God is so caring. Once he has surpassed your wildest dreams, don't forget him. Too many forget God when they are blessed with prosperity and only remember him when they have strayed from the right path and need God to get them out of trouble.

> When the Lord your God brings you into the land he swore to your fathers, to Abraham, Isaac and Jacob, to give you—a land with large, flourishing cities you did not build, houses filled with all kinds of good things you did not provide, wells you did not dig, and vineyards and olive groves you did not plant—then when you eat and are satisfied, be careful that you do not forget the Lord, who brought you out of Egypt, out of the land of slavery.
>
> Deuteronomy 6:10–12 (NIV)

December 22—Marriage Is God's Gift

Just knowing that you are loved unconditionally by another person is reason enough to be happy for the rest of your life. Unfortunately many are not content in the bonds of matrimony. Some people are touchy, others are selfish, and others are insecure. Put these shortcomings together, and you have a recipe for discord. That is why all marriages must be set on the foundation of the Rock—Jesus. When we take our gripes before the Lord and our spouse, keeping the lines of communication open and peaceable, then we stand a chance to be truly happy in the arms of our betrothed.

> For this reason a man will leave his father and mother and be united to his wife, and they will become one flesh.
>
> Genesis 2:24 (NIV)

December 23— Doing Good in the Face of Evil

It is tempting to use evil to fight evil, but only goodness can truly defeat the powers of darkness.

> Do not be overcome by evil, but overcome evil with good.
>
> Romans 12:21 (NIV)

December 24—Hypocrites

If your religion is skin deep, you're only cheating yourself.

> And when you pray, do not be like the hypocrites, for they love to pray standing in the synagogues and on the street corners to be seen by men. I tell you the truth, they have received their reward in full.
>
> Matthew 6:5 (NIV)

December 25—True Religion

Real happiness comes from knowing and following God's individualized plan for your life, which is not necessarily the career path that pays the most.

But godliness with contentment is great gain.

1 Timothy 6:6 (NIV)

December 26—Rewards

God doesn't reward fair-weather Christians as much as he rewards the ones who stand up for the truth in a world plagued by lies and corruption. If you're going to devote yourself to God, you're going to have to really mean it. You'll have to fight against the current of society's norms and even against your own natural inclination toward sin. It's not an easy existence, but God promises us that it's most worthwhile.

> Blessed are you when people insult you, persecute you and falsely say all kinds of evil against you because of me. Rejoice and be glad, because great is your reward in heaven, for in the same way they persecuted the prophets who were before you.
>
> Matthew 5:11–12 (NIV)

December 27—No Escape

Destiny is an amazing thing. Although we have been given the right of freewill, God always gets what he expects, even if his people delay him.

> But Jonah ran away from the LORD and headed for Tarshish. He went down to Joppa, where he found a ship bound for that port. After paying the fare, he went aboard and sailed for Tarshish to flee from the LORD.
>
> Jonah 1:3 (NIV)

December 28—Fear Not

There is no lasting harm anyone can inflict on a truly innocent man.

> When I am afraid, I will trust in you. In God, whose word I praise, in God I trust; I will not be afraid. What can mortal man do to me?
>
> Psalm 56:3–4 (NIV)

December 29—Fairness

God's power is immeasurable, and his goodness immense. He is not tempted to treat his children with undue contempt. He loves us unconditionally, and has the right and authority to do whatever he pleases. In this fact we may take refuge. God is good.

> The Almighty is beyond our reach and exalted in power; in his justice and great righteousness, he does not oppress.
>
> Job 37:23 (NIV)

December 30—Knowledge

To know the scriptures in the Bible is to have an understanding of the power of God. That understanding will give you the strength to handle all difficult circumstances.

> Jesus replied, "You are in error because you do not know the Scriptures or the power of God."
>
> Matthew 22:29 (NIV)

December 31—Our Refuge

As you observe New Year's Eve tonight, consider it a holy holiday meant for you to take a meaningful moral inventory of what your life was like this year. Are you proud or disappointed? What can you do differently next year? Our refuge is God, and he will always answer our prayers when they come from a pure motive. Just ask him for understanding and a willingness to improve.

> God is our refuge and strength, an ever-present help in trouble.
>
> Psalm 46:1 (NIV)